بِسم اللّٰه الرّحمن الرّحِيم

IN THE NAME OF ALLĀH, THE MERCIFUL, THE COMPASSIONATE.

اَللّٰهُمَّ صَلِّ عَلٰى سَيِّدِنَا مُحَمَّدٍ ۞ الْفَاتِحِ لِمَا أُغْلِقَ ۞ وَالْخَاتِمِ لِمَا سَبَقَ ۞ نَاصِرِ الْحَقِّ بِالْحَقِّ ۞ وَالْهَادِى إِلٰى صِرَاطِكَ الْمُسْتَقِيمِ ۞ وَ عَلٰى آلِهِ حَقَّ قَدْرِهِ وَمِقْدَارِهِ الْعَظِيمِ ۞

"Oh Allāh! Send salutations upon our master Muhammad. The opener of what was closed.
The seal of what had preceded. The helper of the truth by the truth. The guide to Your straight path.
May Allah send salutations upon his family according to his greatness and magnificent rank."

The purpose of this book is to introduce beginner students to the sacred science of tajwīd, particularly its practical application. The presentation of the Qurānic text in this book is in line with the 'South African' 13-line Qurān print, as it is most convenient especially for non-Arab learners.

Having taught tajwīd for over a decade, I have developed methods and techniques along the way to help aspiring students who wish to learn how to recite the Qurān correctly.

I am incredibly indebted and grateful to my beloved teachers, especially Hāfidh Ali (حفظه الله), as well as my family, friends, colleagues, and students who have assisted in the compilation of this book.

Tajwīd must be studied under the tutelage of a qualified teacher. Books, pre-recorded lessons, blogs, and other resources serve only as supplementary guides. They do not suffice as adequate substitutes to a teacher. It is an absolute necessity for all students to recite to, and receive feedback from a teacher in order to make corrections.

The Qurān has been inherited through generations by way of oral tradition with an intimate student-teacher relationship.

This book has been designed by Qurānic Insights, who provide free monthly tajwīd classes for beginners online, as well as many other courses and webinars.

To find out more about Qurānic Insights' various other projects, please refer to the information provided on the last page of this book.

I pray that Allāh accepts and grants immense barakah in our endeavours to attain closeness to Him. Āmīn!

AbdulHayy Salloo
Qurānic Insights
www.QuranicInsights.com

Qurānic Insights | Level 1 Tajwīd Intensive | Guided Reading

Contents

Tajwīd

Meaning of Tajwīd:

Tajwīd literally means, "to improve (something)". In the context of reciting the Holy Qurān, tajwīd is the science of pronouncing the correct articulation points of the Arabic letters as well as applying certain rules specific to the speech of Allāh throughout the Qurān.

Obligation and Importance of Tajwīd:

Allāh says in the Qurān: وَرَتِّلِ الْقُرْآنَ تَرْتِيلًا

"And recite the Qurān with measured recitation".
(Surah al-Muzzammil, 73:4)

Alī ibn Abī Ṭālib (RA) said in the explanation of this āyah:
"Al-Tartīl is Tajwīd of the letters and knowing where to stop [correctly]".
(Al-Nashr of Ibn Al-Jazarī 209:1)

Umm Salamah (RA) was asked about the recitation of the Prophet ﷺ, which she described as a recitation "clearly distinguished letter by letter".
(Al-Tirmidhi)

Laḥn Jalī: 'Clear major mistakes'
Any mistake that changes the meaning intended by Allāh would be regarded as laḥn jalī. This includes:

- Mispronunciation of letters.
- Lengthening short vowels or shortening long vowels.
- Changing vowels.

Laḥn Khafī: 'Minor mistakes'
Any mistake pertaining to the rules specific to the Qurān is considered laḥn khafī. This includes anything that contributes to the completeness and beauty of the recitation.

Makhraj:
Makhraj literally means, "A place of exit". In the context of the Qurān, it is where sound is articulated from. To pronounce each and every letter from its distinct articulation point, giving each letter its unique rights and dues of characteristics.

1.1: Arabic Alphabet

Learning Objectives:

- **Recognise** each letter.
- **Pronounce** each letter correctly.
- **Makhraj** – understand and explain the articulation point of each letter.

	١
	ب
	ت
	ث
	ج
	ح
	خ

	د
	ذ
	ر
	ز
	س
	ش
	ص

	ض
	ط
	ظ
	ع
	غ
	ف
	ق

	ك
	ل
	م
	ن
	ه
	و
	ي

	ء
	ة

1.2: Makhārij

Letter	Makhraj	English Equivalent	Further Description & Tips
ا	Emptiness of the mouth	"N**aa**n"	The sound of Alif cannot be initiated by itself.
ب	Moist parts of the lips	"**Ba**t", "**Ba**nk"	Letter 'B' sound
ت	Tip of the tongue touching the roots of the top two teeth	"Sies**ta**", "S**ta**nd" (Not like "**Ta**n")	A softer and subtle 'T' sound
ث	Tip of the tongue touching the edge of the **top two teeth only**	"**Tha**nk", "**Th**under", "**Th**irst", "**Th**ink"	Position the tongue to the Makhraj <u>before</u> attempting the sound.
ج	Raising the middle of the tongue, touching the top palate	"**Jee**p", "**G**ym"	A stronger letter 'J' sound. Avoid French pronunciation
ح	Tightening the muscles of the **middle of the throat**	"A**ha**!" (Exclamation)	A sigh or panting sound **- Throat Letter**
خ	Tightening the muscles of the **top of the throat**	"Lo**ch**" (Scottish pronunciation)	Rough scratchy sound, as if clearing your throat. **- Heavy Letter** (See pg. 11) **- Throat Letter**
د	Tip of the tongue touching the roots of the top two teeth	"Hea**d**", "S**quad**"	A softer and subtle 'D' sound
ذ	Tip of the tongue touching the edge of the **top two teeth only**	"**Tha**t", "**Th**ose", "**Th**e", "**Th**is"	Position the tongue to the Makhraj <u>before</u> attempting the sound.
ر	Tip of the tongue <u>hitting</u> the top palate whilst raising the back of the tongue	"**Ro**bert", "**Ro**ck"	A strong letter 'R' sound (See pg. 11)
ز	Teeth closed, tongue touching the edge of the <u>bottom two teeth only</u>	"**Za**p", "Fi**zz**", "Bu**zz**", "Pu**zz**le"	An emphasised buzzing sound.
س	Teeth closed, tongue touching the edge of the <u>bottom two teeth only</u>	"**S**cene", "**Se**ed"	Letter 'S' sound
ش	Raising the middle of the tongue touching the top palate	"**Sh**een", "**Shee**p"	A strong "Shh!" sound
ص	Tip of the tongue pushing firmly against the edge of the **bottom two teeth only** whilst <u>raising the back of the tongue</u>	(Heavier version of the letter س)	**- Heavy Letter** (See pg. 11)
ض	The back edge of the tongue (either left or right side, or both) pushing firmly against <u>the side teeth</u> whilst <u>raising the back of the tongue</u>	N/A	**- Heavy Letter** (See pg. 11)

Letter	Articulation	Example	Notes
ط	Tip of the tongue pushing firmly against the roots of the top two teeth whilst <u>raising the back of the tongue</u>	(Heavier version of the letter ت)	- **Heavy Letter** (See pg. 11)
ظ	Tip of the tongue pushing firmly against the edge of the **top two teeth only** whilst <u>raising the back of the tongue</u>	(Heavier version of the letter ذ)	Position the tongue to the Makhraj <u>before</u> attempting the sound. - **Heavy Letter** (See pg. 11)
ع	Tightening the muscles of the **<u>middle of the throat</u>**	N/A	Pulling the tongue backwards in reverse helps to tighten and squeeze the throat - **Throat Letter**
غ	Tightening the muscles of the **top of the throat**	"**R**estau**r**ant" (French pronunciation) Pronounced like a throaty French 'R', incorporating a letter 'G' sound.	Gargling sound. - Beginning of the throat, make the base of the tongue thicker and push the tongue against the lower teeth. - **Heavy Letter** (See pg. 11) - **Throat Letter**
ف	Top teeth touching the inner bottom lower lip	"**Fa**n", "**Fa**shion"	Letter 'F' sound
ق	Lifting the farthest back end of the tongue	N/A	Sound of a crow - **Heavy Letter** (See pg. 11)
ك	Back end of the tongue (not as far back as the letter ق)	"S**c**out", "S**ca**m". "So**cc**er" (U.S pronunciation)	This letter does **not** make a typical 'K'. Compare the subtle difference in the words "Si**kh**" & "See**k**"
ل	Tip of the tongue touching the top palate	"**Lam**b", "**La**nd"	Letter 'L' sound
م	Drier parts of the lips	"**Me**me", "**Me**"	Letter 'M' sound
ن	Tip of the tongue touching the top palate	"**Noo**dles"	Letter 'N' sound
و	Outer parts of the lips	"**Wow**", "**Wa**ffle"	Letter 'W' sound
ه	**<u>Bottom of the throat</u>**	"**Ha**nd", "**Ha**zy"	A soft breathing sound - **Throat Letter**
ي	Raising the middle of the tongue touching the top palate	"**Ya**p", "**Ya**m"	A stronger letter 'Y' sound
ء	**<u>Bottom of the throat</u>**	"**U**p", "**U**nder"	A glottal stop, like when a native English speaker drops the letter '<u>T</u>' in words such as 'Ca<u>t</u>', 'Po<u>t</u>', 'Ma<u>tt</u>er' Ca**'**, Po**'**, Ma**'**er - **Throat Letter**

2: Supporting Notes | Heavy Letters & Throat Letters

- **TASK** - Memorise all 7 Heavy Letters – خ ص ض ط ظ غ ق

<u>How to recite the heavy Letters – 4 Points to remember</u> **(RASF).**

1. **R**aise the back end of the tongue.
2. **A**pply pressure on the makhraj.
3. **S**low release of the sound.
4. **F**ull Mouth – A build-up of air inside the mouth.

Please note – regarding the Letter ر:

Although the default pronunciation of the letter ر is heavy,

it is **not** considered amongst the group of heavy letters.
(This is because it is pronounced as a "light" letter in some instances, such as when holding a kasrah. Refer to page 20)

- **TASK** - Memorise all 6 Throat Letters, along with their specific

makhraj – خ غ ح ع ه ء

TOP	6. خ	5. غ
MIDDLE	4. ح	3. ع
BOTTOM	2. ه	1. ء

Exercise:

- Draw a circle under all the heavy letters, as shown in the first example.
- Independently be able to identify and pronounce all the letters correctly.
- Explain the makhraj of each letter.

ج	و	غ	ه	ضْ
ف	ء	ث	خ	س
ك	ظ	ش	د	ع
ص	ب	م	ز	ط
خ	ق	ت¹	رْ	ح
ي	ذ	ن	غ	ل
ل	خ	ض	ا	ص
ظ	س	ب	ه	ق

¹ The letter ر , by default, is pronounced heavily. Therefore, put a circle below it to remind you to recite it heavily.
*(Although, remember it is not officially from amongst the group of heavy letters)

3.1: Ḥarakah – Short Vowel | Fatḥah

3 Types of Harakāt: 1. Fatḥah ٌ   2. Kasrah ٍ   3. Ḍammah ٌ

Arabic Alphabet with Fatḥah

The fatḥah is pronounced by opening the mouth upwards with a slight smile.
(Up – ~~App~~   Bun – ~~Ban~~)

1. Keep short – do not lengthen   **2.** Recite smoothly – no abrupt endings*

			1
ثَ	تَ	بَ	اَ
دَ	خَ	حَ	جَ
سَ	زَ	رَ 2	ذَ
طَ	ضَ	صَ	شَ
فَ	غَ	عَ	ظَ
مَ	لَ	كَ	قَ
يَ	وَ	ةَ	نَ

* If the letters with any Harakāt are read with an abrupt ending, that would mean you're adding an extra letter ء at the end of it. Therefore, that would be incorrect. (Refer to the first example on pg. 26)

¹ The letter Alif - When the Alif holds any ḥarakah, such as a Fatḥah, it is considered to be a ء instead – Not an Alif.

² The letter Rā' – Although it is not amongst the 7 heavy letters, when it holds a Fatḥah, you pronounce it heavy. Thus, we will put a circle underneath it.

Words with Fatḥah

- Before attempting any word, you must first **draw a small circle** under the **heavy letters** to remind you to pronounce the letter heavy. Whilst the remaining letters will be light. (See example below)

- Follow along and listen carefully to how the teacher demonstrates the letter-by-letter breakdown of the word examples:

"اَخَذَ" : اَ – خَ – اَخَ – ذَ = اَخَذَ

*You must **always** practice using this same breakdown method.

End	Middle	Beginning	The Letter
ذَ رَ اَ	سَ اَ لَ	اَ خَ ذَ	اَ
ذَرَاَ	سَاَلَ	اَخَذَ	
ذَ ةَ بَ	صَ بَ رَ	بَ دَ اَ	بَ
ذَهَبَ	صَبَرَ	بَدَاَ	
سَ كَ تَ	فَ تَ حَ	تَ رَ كَ	تَ
سَكَتَ	فَتَحَ	تَرَكَ	
شَ جَ رَ ةَ	– – –	– – –	ةَ
شَجَرَةَ			

End	Middle	Beginning	The Letter
بَ عَ ثَ	مَ ثَ لَ	ثَ مَ رَ	ثَ
بَعَثَ	مَثَلَ	ثَمَرُ	
مَ رَ جَ	وَ جَ دَ	جَ مَ عَ	جَ
مَرَجَ	وَجَدَ	جَمَعَ	
شَ رَ حَ	اَ حَ دَ	حَ مَ لَ	حَ
شَرَحَ	اَحَدَ	حَمَلَ	
وَ نَ فَ خَ	دَ خَ لَ	خَ تَ مَ	خَ
وَنَفَخَ	دَخَلَ	خَتَمَ	
حَ سَ دَ	صَ دَ قَ	دَ خَ لَ	دَ
حَسَدَ	صَدَقَ	دَخَلَ	
نَ بَ ذَ	كَ ذَ بَ	ذَ ہَ بَ	ذَ
نَبَذَ	كَذَبَ	ذَهَبَ	

End	Middle	Beginning	The Letter
حَ ضَ رَ	تَ رَ كَ	رَ جَ عَ	رَ
حَضَرَ	تَرَكَ	رَجَعَ	
لَ بَ رَ زَ	عَ زَ مَ	زَ عَ مَ	زَ
لَبَرَزَ	عَزَمَ	زَعَمَ	
عَ بَ سَ	كَ سَ بَ	سَ رَ قَ	سَ
عَبَسَ	كَسَبَ	سَرَقَ	
_ _ _	كَ شَ فَ	شَ كَ رَ	شَ
	كَشَفَ	شَكَرَ	
نَ كَ صَ	فَ صَ لَ	صَ دَ قَ	صَ
نَكَصَ	فَصَلَ	صَدَقَ	
فَ رَ ضَ	حَ ضَ رَ	ضَ رَ بَ	ضَ
فَرَضَ	حَضَرَ	ضَرَبَ	

End	Middle	Beginning	The Letter
بَ سَ طَ	فَ طَ رَ	طَ بَ عَ	طَ
بَسَطَ	فطَرَ	طَبَعَ	
ــــ	نَ ظَ رَ	ظَ لَ مَ	ظَ
	نَظَرَ	ظَلَمَ	
شَ رَ عَ	جَ عَ لَ	عَ بَ دَ	عَ
شَرَعَ	جَعَلَ	عَبَدَ	
نَ زَ غَ	فَ غَ فَ رَ	غَ فَ رَ	غَ
نَزَغَ	فَغَفَرَ	غَفَرَ	
صَ رَ فَ	اَ فَ لَ	فَ صَ لَ	فَ
صَرَفَ	اَفَلَ	فَصَلَ	
اَ بَ قَ	تَ قَ عَ	قَ تَ لَ	قَ
اَبَقَ	تَقَعَ	قَتَلَ	

End	Middle	Beginning	The Letter
تَ رَ كَ	اَ كَ لَ	كَ تَ بَ	كَ
تَرَكَ	اَكَلَ	كَتَبَ	
نَ زَ لَ	سَ لَ فَ	لَ عَ نَ	لَ
نَزَلَ	سَلَفَ	لَعَنَ	
حَ كَ مَ	اَ مَ رَ	مَ نَ عَ	مَ
حَكَمَ	اَمَرَ	مَنَعَ	
سَ كَ نَ	مَ نَ عَ	نَ بَ ذَ	نَ
سَكَنَ	مَنَعَ	نَبَذَ	
___	جَ هَ رَ	ةَ لَ كَ	ةَ
	جَهَرَ	هَلَكَ	
___	فَ وَ هَ بَ	وَ سَ قَ	وَ
	فَوَهَبَ	وَسَقَ	

End	Middle	Beginning	The Letter
_ _ _	وَ يَ ذَ رَ كَ	يَ دَ كَ	يَ
	وَيَذَرَكَ	يَدَكَ	

3.1.a: Special Letters!

The 6 special letters are:

ا د ذ ر ز و

There are 6 letters in the Arabic alphabet that never connect onto letters
that appear immediately after them within the same word.
(Analyse the examples in the middle columns above again to understand this rule well)

- Continue to practice using the letter-by-letter breakdown method.
You **must** note down any rules before attempting each and every example.

"خَلَقَ" : خَ – لَ – خَلَ – قَ = خَلَقَ

وَضَعَ	وَقَبَ	سَكَنَ	خَلَقْ
شَجَرَ	تَرَكَ	نَكَصَ	حَسَدَ
نَزَعَ	جَمَعَ	ظَلَمَ	بَسَطَ
حَضَرَ	بَعَثَ	ذَهَبَ	اَبَقَ

3.2: Ḥarakah – Short Vowel | Kasrah

Arabic Alphabet with Kasrah

The kasrah is pronounced by lowering the jaw.

1. Keep Short – do not lengthen   **2.** Recite Smoothly – no abrupt endings

(In – ~~End~~   Bin – ~~Ben~~)

ثِ	تِ	بِ	اِ
دِ	خِ*	حِ	جِ
سِ	زِ	رِ	ذِ
طِ	ضِ	صِ	شِ
فِ	غِ*	عِ	ظِ
مِ	لِ	كِ	قِ*
يِ	وِ	هِ	نِ

* قِ, غِ, خِ – These letters with a kasrah reduce in heaviness.

- #4 of **RAS**F (~~Reduce the build-up of air inside the mouth~~)

Words with Kasrah

- Continue to **draw a small circle** under the **Heavy Letters** to remind you to pronounce the letter heavy.

- Do not circle the letters خِ , غِ , قِ as they reduce in heaviness.

- The letter رِ (with a Kasrah) is pronounced Lightly.

"اِرَمَ" : اِ – رَ – اِرَ – مَ = اِرَمَ

Example	The Letter	Example	The Letter	Example	The Letter
اَ بَ تِ	تِ	خَ بِ طَ	بِ	اِ رَ مَ ○	اِ
اَبَتِ		حَبِطَ		اِرَمَ ○	
رَ حِ مَ	حِ	تَ جِ دَ	جِ	وَ رَثَ ةِ	ةِ
رَحِمَ		تَجِدَ		وَرَثَةِ	
اَ ذِ نَ	ذِ	رَ دِ فَ	دِ	بَ خِ لَ	خِ
اَذِنَ		رَدِفَ		بَخِلَ	
خَ سِ رَ	سِ	فَ فَ زِعَ	زِ	اَ ثَ رِ	رِ
خَسِرَ		فَفَزِعَ		اَثَرِ	

Example	The Letter	Example	The Letter	Example	The Letter
خَ طِ فَ	طِ	رَ ضِ يَ	ضِ	شِ يَ ةَ	شِ
خَطِفَ		رَضِيَ		شِيَةَ	
بَ قِ يَ	قِ	حَ فِ ظَ	فِ	عِ وَ جَ	عِ
بَقِي		حَفِظَ		عِوَجَ	
اَ مِ نَ	مِ	عَ لِ مَ	لِ	مَ لِ كِ	كِ
اَمِنَ		عَلِمَ		مَلِكِ	
وَ لَ وِ	وِ	شَ هِ دَ	هِ	تَ رَ نِ	نِ
وَلَوِ		شَهِدَ		تَرَنِ	

يَدَي   بِبَدَنِكَ   تَزِدِ   وَاِذ

بِثَمَرِهِ   خَشِيَ   بِعِصَمِ   شِيَعَ

تَقِ   لِاَهَبَ   عَمِلَ   يَئِسَ

3.3: Ḥarakah – Short Vowel | Ḍammah

Arabic Alphabet with Ḍammah

Ḍammah is pronounced by rounding the lips without letting them come into complete contact.

1. Keep Short – Do not lengthen   **2.** Recite Smoothly – No abrupt ending

(Book – ~~Born~~   Took – ~~Talk~~)

ثُ	تُ	بُ	اُ
دُ	خُ ○	حُ	جُ
سُ	زُ	رُ ○	ذُ
طُ ○	ضُ ○	صُ ○	شُ
فُ	غُ ○	عُ	ظُ ○
مُ	لُ	كُ	قُ ○
يُ	وُ	هُ	نُ

¹ The letter Rā' – Although it is not amongst the 7 heavy letters, when it holds a Ḍammah, you pronounce it heavy. Thus, we will put a circle underneath it.

Example	The Letter	Example	The Letter	Example	The Letter
تُ طِ عَ تُطِعِ	تُ	خَ بُ ثَ خَبُثَ	بُ	أُ فِ كَ أُفِكَ	أُ
حُ شِ رَ حُشِرَ	حُ	يَ لِ جُ يَلِجُ	جُ	نَ رِ ثُ نَرِثُ	ثُ
اُ ذُ نُ اُذُنُ	ذُ	اَحَ دُ اَحَدُ	دُ	خُ لِ قَ خُلِقَ	خُ
رُ سُ لُ رُسُلُ	سُ	زُ بُ رِ زُبُرِ	زُ	اَتَ ذَرُ اَتَذَرُ	رُ
فَ طُ بِ عَ فَطُبِعَ	طُ	ضُ رِ بَ ضُرِبَ	ضُ	صُ حُ فِ صُحُفِ	صُ

- Continue to practice using the letter-by-letter breakdown method.
You **must** note down any rules before attempting each and every example.

"صُحُفِ" : صُ - حُ - صُحُ - فِ = صُحُفِ

"ظُلِمَ" : ظُ – لِ – ظُلِ – مَ = ظُلِمَ

Example	The Letter	Example	The Letter	Example	The Letter
غُ لِ بَ تْ غُلِبَتِ	غُ	عُ ثِ رَ عُثِرَ	عُ	ظُ لِ مَ ظُلِمَ	ظُ
كُ بِ تَ كُبِتَ	كُ	خُ لُ قُ خُلُقُ	قُ	تَ صِ فُ تَصِفُ	فُ
أُ ذُ نُ أُذُنُ	نُ	غُ نَ مُ غَنَمُ	مُ	لُ عِ نَ لُعِنَ	لُ
يُ رِ دِ يُرِدِ	يُ	وُ ضِ عَ وُضِعَ	وُ	هُ وَ هُوَ	ءُ

ذُبِحَ	ضَعُفَ	قُرِئَ فَقُتِلَ
ثُلُثِ	خُلُقُ	رُسُلُ عُنُقِكَ
فَبَصَرُكَ	حَصَبُ	صُحُفِ أَعِظُكَ

4: Sukūn

Arabic Letters with Sukūn ْ

A letter with a sukūn (literally: "stationary") doesn't have *movement* like the harakāt (vowels) do.
The sākinah letter must be joined/read with the letter before it that has a ḥarakah (vowel).

	ثُ		*تْ		*بْ		أْ
يَثْ	تَثْ	يْتْ	تَتْ	يَبْ	تَبْ	يَأْ	تَأْ
	*دْ		خْ		حْ		*جْ
يَدْ	تَدْ	يَخْ	تَخْ	يَحْ	تَحْ	يَجْ	تَجْ
	سْ		زْ		رْ		ذْ
يَسْ	تَسْ	يَزْ	تَزْ	يَرْ	تَرْ	يَذْ	تَذْ
	*طْ		ضْ		صْ		شْ
يَطْ	تَطْ	يَضْ	تَضْ	يَصْ	تَصْ	يَشْ	تَشْ
	فْ		غْ		عْ		ظْ
يَفْ	تَفْ	يَغْ	تَغْ	يَعْ	تَعْ	يَظْ	تَظْ
	مْ		لْ		*كْ		*قْ
يَمْ	تَمْ	يَلْ	تَلْ	يَكْ	تَكْ	يَقْ	تَقْ
	يْ		وْ		ةْ		نْ
يَيْ	تَيْ	يَوْ	تَوْ	يَهْ	تَهْ	يَنْ	تَنْ

- Heavy/Light & Light/Heavy Combinations. When a Light Letter joins onto a Heavy Letter, or vice versa, be mindful not to transfer the quality of one letter onto the other.

* See the next page for the relevant rules.

5.1: Qalqalah – Bouncing Sound

دُ جْ بْ طْ قْ

When any of these letters contain a sukūn, you must recite them with a Bouncing Sound.

*Remember to keep the bounce Heavy for the Heavy Letters (قْ طْ)

[Practice: 7.1 – Pg. 31]

5.2: Hams – *"Tick and a Click"* – Sharp Breathing Sound

تْ كْ

When any of these letters have a sukūn, you must recite them with a sharp breathing sound - *with a "Tick and a Click."*

The pronunciation in this scenario will be slightly different to how they are usually pronounced with a vowel, as it brings out a
1. Strong stoppage of the sound whilst   2. Exhaling/breathing out.

*Be mindful not to do qalqalah on these letters.

كْ	تْ
The letter ك is not usually pronounced like a 'K' sound. The **only time** the ك makes a 'K' sound is when it has a **sukūn**.	The letter ت is not usually pronounced like a 'T' sound exactly. The **only time** the ت makes a 'T' sound is when it has a **sukūn**.

[Practice: 7.2 – Pg. 31]

6: The Letter ر "Rā'" Rule & Quick Review

رَ / رُ = Heavy   رِ = Light

- If the ر has a sukūn, then the ḥarakah before it will determine whether it is

Heavy or Light.

تَرْ / تُرْ = Heavy   تِرْ = Light

- **TASK** – Quick Review!
  Please Note:
  - You **must** have all these rules memorised and
  - You **must** be able to appropriately annotate each rule accordingly.

Rules	Annotations
1. 7 Heavy Letters – خ ص ض ط ظ غ ق	O
(خِ, غِ, قِ – Reduces in Heaviness)	N/A
2. 6 Throat Letters - ء ه ع ح غ خ	N/A
3.a. Letter ر Rule – Fatḥah / Ḍammah = (Heavy)	O
3.b. Kasrah = Light	N/A
4. Sukūn	تَسْ
5. 5 Qalqalah Letters - قُ طْ بْ جْ دْ	Q
6. 2 Hams Letters – كُ تْ	H

7: Words with Sukūn

- Continue to practice these examples with the same breakdown method.
Any letters joined with the sukūn must be spelt & read together. For example:

$$" يَأۡمَنُ " : يَأۡ - مَ - يَأۡمَ - نُ - نُ = يَأۡمَنُ $$

You **must** note down any rules before attempting each and every example.

- Annotations: (See examples below)

Heavy Letter – **O**   Qalqalah – **Q**   Hams – **H**   Sukūn -

Example at the end	The Letter	Examples In words	The Letter
يَشَأۡ	شَأۡ	يَأۡمَنُ	يَأۡ
يَتُبۡ	تُبۡ	تُبۡتَ	تُبۡ **Q**
فَيَمُتۡ	مُتۡ	فَٱتۡبَعَ	ٱتۡ **H**
تَحۡنَثۡ	نَثۡ	فَلَبِثۡتَ	بِثۡ
يَخۡرُجۡ	رُجۡ	فَٱجۡرُ	ٱجۡ
تَفۡرَحۡ	رَحۡ	زُحۡزِحَ	رُحۡ
نَنۡسَخۡ	سَخۡ	تَخۡلُقُ	تَخۡ
أَعۡهَدۡ	هَدۡ	تُدۡهِنُ	تُدۡ
فَخُذۡ	خُذۡ	عُذۡتُ	عُذۡ
تَقۡهَرۡ	هَرۡ	تُرۡجَعُ	تُرۡ
_ _ _	_ _ _	كَنزۡتُمۡ	نزۡ

Example at the end	The Letter	Examples In words	The Letter
نَقْتَبِسْ	بِسْ	تَسْطَعْ	تَسْ
‐ ‐ ‐	‐ ‐ ‐	اَشْهَدُ	اَشْ
تَحْرِصْ	رِصْ	تَصْبِرُ	تَصْ
تُعْرِضْ	رِضْ	بِضْعَ	بِضْ
فَاَسْقِطْ	قِطْ	بِبَطْنٍ	بَطْ
‐ ‐ ‐	‐ ‐ ‐	اَوَعَظْتَ	عَظْ
تُطِعْ	طِعْ	بُعْثِرَ	بُعْ
تُرِغْ	نِغْ	فَيُغْرِقَكُمْ	يُغْ
تَخَفْ	خَفْ	اَفْرِغْ	اَفْ
فَلْيُنْفِقْ	فِقْ	تَقْهَرْ	تَقْ
تُشْرِكُ	رِكُ	تُكْرِهُ	تُكْ
تَقُلْ	قُلْ	اَعَجِلْتُمْ	جِلْ
خَلَقَكُمْ	كُمْ	فَاَقَمْتَ	قَمْ
فَاَذَنْ	ذَنْ	تَنْهَرْ	تَنْ
اَرْجِهْ	جِهْ	جَهْدَ	جَهْ
اَغَيْرَ	غَيْ	تَوْجَلْ	تَوْ

7.1 Words with Qalqalah

Examples at the[1] end of words	Examples in the middle of words	Examples in the middle of words	Qalqalah Letter
وَارْزُقْ	خَلَقْنَ	اَقْبِلْ	قْ
فَاهْبِطْ	يَطْهُرْنَ	شَطْرَ	طْ
يَتُبْ	قِبْلَةَ	صُبْحِ	بْ
يُخْرِجْ	اَتَجْعَلُ	وَجْهِكَ	جْ
لَقَدْ	فَادْعُ	سِدْرَةٍ	دْ

[1] When qalqalah occurs at the end of words, the strength of the bounce will be slightly stronger than when it appears in the middle of words.

7.2 Words with Hams

كَتَبَتْ	فَاَخَذَتْكُمْ	ضُرِبَتْ	تْ
وَالْفِتْنَةُ	قَسَتْ	فَانْفَجَرَتْ	تْ
تَكْتُمُ	يَكْتُبُ	وَاسْتَكْبَرَ	كْ
كَذِكْرِكُمْ	وَالْحِكْمَةَ	يَكْفُرُ	كْ

Hams – The quality of hams also occurs on some other letters. The reason why we have only introduced the تْ & كْ in the book, is because the other letters will naturally have the sharp breathing sound when recited.

Whereas the تْ & كْ require extra attention when trying to pronounce with the quality of hams.

صَب ثَ رَت دَب تَت بَب

نَخْ خَ خَّ حَ جَّ جَّ جَ حَثْ

عَز مَر زَز تَّ رَز ذَّ دَّ رَخْ

غَض ضَض قَص صَص غَش

يَغْ مَع حَظ ظَظ قَطْ طَطْ

مَكْ كَكْ رَقْ قَّ فَّ إِذْ

حَوْ بَي فَوْ سَوْ كَي يَي وَوْ

عَنْهُ وَاَهْدِيكَ يَوْمَ نَجْعَلْ اَلَمْ

فَسَوۡفَ   وَٱلۡقَتۡ   وَٱذِنَتۡ   عَلَيۡهِ   وَلَقَدۡ

اَفۡلَحَ   يَعۡلَمُ   اَخۡرَجَ   اَمۡهِلۡهُمۡ   اُقۡسِمُ

فَدَمۡدَمَ   اَهۡلَكۡتُ   يَقۡدِرَ   رِزۡقَ   كَيۡفَ

تَتۡرُكُهُ   وِزۡرَكَ   يُخۡلَقۡ   عِلۡمٍ   فَاَيۡنَ   تَقۡهَرۡ

فَاَثَرۡنَ   اَخۡلَدَ   تَنۡهَرۡ   سُطِحَتۡ   بِقَوۡلِ

نَصۡرُ   اَعۡبُدُ   وَاَخۡرَجَتۡ   تُطِعۡهُ   فَلۡيَدۡعُ

سَوۡطَ   فِرۡعَوۡنَ   وَاَرۡسَلَ   بِحَمۡدِ   وَرَاَيۡتَ

غَيۡرُ   اَحۡسَنِ   فَرَغۡتَ   ذِكۡرَكَ   ظَهۡرَكَ

يَعۡلَمُ   فَوَسَطۡنَ   زُلۡزِلَتۡ   مَطۡلَعِ   بِاِذۡنِ

8.1: Long Vowels - Ḥurūf al-Madd

3 types of Ḥurūf al-Madd

1. "Fatḥah before Alif"   - (◌ Long Fatḥah)

2. "Kasrah before Yā' Sākin"   - (◌ Long Kasrah)

3. "Ḍammah before Wāw Sākin"   - (◌ Long Ḍammah)

Arabic letters with Alif Madd

- For practice purposes, we will be elongating Ḥurūf Madd longer than we normally would.

Alif Madd	The Letter	Alif Madd	The Letter	Alif Madd	The Letter	Alif Madd	The Letter
ثَا	ثَ	تَا	تَ	بَا	بَ	اٖ - ءَا	ءَ
دَا	دَ	خَا	خَ	حَا	حَ	جَا	جَ
سَا	سَ	زَا	زَ	رَا	رَ	ذَا	ذَ
طَا	طَ	ضَا	ضَ	صَا	صَ	شَا	شَ
فَا	فَ	غَا	غَ	عَا	عَ	ظَا	ظَ
مَا	مَ	لَا	لَ	كَا	كَ	قَا	قَ
يَا	يَ	وَا	وَ	هَا	هَ	نَا	نَ

Annotation: underline every instance of Alif Harf Madd (as shown below)

Example in the end	Example in the middle	Example in the beginning	The Madd Letter
رَاىٰ	بِاٰلِهَتِنَا	اٰدَمُ	ءَا - اٰ
اَبٰى	تَبٰرَكَ	بَادِيَ	بَا
اَتٰى	وَالْيَتٰمٰى	تَابَ	تَا
اُنْثٰى	مَثَانِيَ	ثَالِثُ	ثَا
سَبْحٰى	وَيُجَادِلُ	جَامِعُ	جَا
وَاَصْلَحَا	يُحَادِدْ	حٰجَجْتُمْ	حَا
اَخَا	تَخَاصُمُ	خٰدِعُهُمْ	خَا
هَدٰى	جَاهَدْكَ	دَابِرَ	دَا
اَذَا	فَذَاقَتْ	ذَاتَ	ذَا
تَتْرَا	فَخَرَاجُ	رَابِعُهُمْ	رَا
لِتُجْزٰى	زِلْزَالَهَا	زَالَتَا	زَا

Example in the end	Example in the middle	Example in the beginning	The Madd Letter
عَسٰى	حِسَابٌ	فَسَالَتْ	سَا
يَغْشٰى	تَشَابَهَتْ	شَانِئَكَ	شَا
وَعَصٰى	اَصَبْتَهُمْ	صَاحِبَ	صَا
يَرْضٰى	مَضَاجِعِهِمْ	ضَاقَتْ	ضَا
اَعْطٰى	سُلْطٰنُهُ	طَاقَةَ	طَا
لَظٰى	عِظَامٌ	ظَهِرُ	ظَا
يَسْعٰى	طَعَامٌ	عِلْمٌ	عَا
يَبْلُغَا	مَغَانِمَ	غَالِبَ	غَا
كَفٰى	يَخْصِفَانِ	فَاتَكُمْ	فَا
فَسَقٰى	نَفَقٰتِهِمْ	قَالَ	قَا
اَزْكٰى	يَكَادُ	كَانَ	كَا

Example in the end	Example in the middle	Example in the beginning	The Madd Letter
سَيَصۡلٰى	صَلَاتَهُمۡ	لَمَسۡتُمۡ	لَا
مَهۡمَا	اَعۡمٰلُهُمۡ	مٰلِكِ	مَا
اَرۡسَلۡنَا	اَعۡطَيۡنٰكَ	نَارُ	نَا
فَوۡقَهَا	اَلۡهٰكُمۡ	هَاؤُمۡ	هَا
هَوٰى	وَتَوَاصَوۡا	وَارِدُهَا	وَا
وَالۡفَيَا	ثِيَابُ	يٰشُعَيۡبُ	يَا

وَلَسَوۡفَ يَرۡضٰى   وَلَا يَخَافُ عُقۡبٰهَا

وَمَا اَدۡرٰىكَ مَا هِيَهۡ   وَهُوَ يَخۡشٰى

اَحۡيَيۡنٰهَا وَاَخۡرَجۡنَا مِنۡهَا   كَانَا يَاۡكُلٰنِ

لَهُمُ الۡاٰيٰتِ   لَا يَتَنَاهَوۡنَ عَنۡ

8.2: Long Vowels - Ḥurūf al-Madd | Yā' Madd

Yā' Madd	The Letter	Yā' Madd	The Letter	Yā' Madd	The Letter	Yā' Madd	The Letter
ثِيْ	ثِ	تِيْ	تِ	بِيْ	بِ	اِيْ	اِ
دِيْ	دِ	خِيْ	خِ	حِيْ	حِ	جِيْ	جِ
سِيْ	سِ	زِيْ	زِ	رِيْ	رِ	ذِيْ	ذِ
طِيْ	طِ	ضِيْ	ضِ	صِيْ	صِ	شِيْ	شِ
فِيْ	فِ	غِيْ	غِ	عِيْ	عِ	ظِيْ	ظِ
مِيْ	مِ	لِيْ	لِ	كِيْ	كِ	قِيْ	قِ
يِيْ	يِ	وِيْ	وِ	هِيْ	ه	نِيْ	نِ

Annotation: underline every instance of Yā' Ḥarf Madd
(as shown on the next page)

- Continue to practice these examples with the same breakdown method. Any letters joined with the sukūn must be spelt & read together. For example:

"اِيْمَانُكُمْ": اِيْ – مَا – اِيْمَا – نُ – اِيْمَانُ – كُمْ = اِيْمَانُكُمْ

You **must** note down any rules before attempting each and every example.

Example in the end	Example in the middle	Example in the beginning	The Madd Letter
دُعَاءِيْ	خَاسِئِيْنَ	اِيْمَانُكُمْ	اِيْ
بِكِتْبِيْ	سَبِيْلِيْ	بِيْ	بِيْ
يَأْتِيْ	يَأْتِيْكُمْ	---	تِيْ
---	تُثِيْرُ	---	ثِيْ
يُزْجِيْ	أُجِيْبُ	جِيْدِهَا	جِيْ
نُصْحِيْ	أُحِيْطَ	حِيْنَ	حِيْ
اَخِيْ	كَخِيْفَتِكُمْ	خِيْفَتِه	خِيْ
وَيَهْدِيْ	حَدِيْثُ	دِيْنِ	دِيْ
لِذِيْ	لِنُذِيْقَهُمْ	ذِيْ	ذِيْ
تَجْرِيْ	يُرِيْدُ	رِيْحُكُمْ	رِيْ
نُجْزِيْ	نَزِيْدَكُمْ	زِيْنَتَكُمْ	زِيْ

Example in the end	Example in the middle	Example in the beginning	The Madd Letter
نَفْسِي	خَمْسِينَ	سِنِينَ	سِي
يُغْشِي	تَشِيعَ	شِيعَتِه	شِي
اَعْصِي	مُخْلِصِينَ	– – –	صِي
اَرْضِي	مُعْرِضِينَ	ضِيزَى	ضِي
اَرَهْطِي	يُعْطِيكَ	– – –	طِي
– – –	حْفِظِينَ	– – –	ظِي
اَقْلِعِي	وَيُعِيدُ	عِيسَى	عِي
اَبْتَغِي	لِيَغِيظَ	وَغِيضَ	غِي
وَتُخْفِي	يَشْفِينِ	فِيهَا	فِي

"وَتُخْفِي" : وَ – تُخْ – فِي = وَتُخْفِي

Example in the end	Example in the middle	Example in the beginning	The Madd Letter
تُبۡقِي	تَقِيكُمۡ	قِيلَ	قِي
وَتَشۡتَكِي	وَاَكِيدُ	– – –	كِي
رُسۡلِي	سَاُصۡلِيهِ	لِي	لِي
تَرۡمِي	جَثِمِينَ	مِيۡرَثُ	مِي
يُجِيرِنِي	يَزۡنِينَ	– – –	نِي
تَشۡتَهِي	يَهِيجُ	– – –	هِي
تَسۡتَوِي	غۡوِينَ	– – –	وِي
يَسۡتَحِۦ	يُحۡيِيكُمۡ	– – –	يِي

"غۡوِينَ" : غۡ – وِي – غۡوِي – نَ = غۡوِينَ

8.2.a: Yā' Madd & Yā' Sākinah

Yā' Madd	Yā' Sākinah	Yā' Madd	Yā' Sākinah
تَشِيعَ	وَعَصَيْنَا	أُجِيبُ	اَيْنَ
مُخْلِصِينَ	قَضَيْتَ	يَأْتِيكُمْ	بَيْنَ
مُعْرِضِينَ	عَيْنَانِ	سَبِيلِي	اَتَيْتَ
يُعْطِيكَ	بِالْغَيْبِ	تُثِيرُ	حَيْثُ
وَيُعِيدُ	اَخْفَيْتُمْ	أُحِيطَ	خَيْرَ
لِيَغِيظَ	لِكَيْ	أَخِيهِ	يَدَيْهِ
يَشْفِينِ	عَلَيْهِ	حَدِيثٌ	يُؤْذَيْنَ
تَقِيكُمْ	هَيْتَ	مَعَاذِيرَهُ	شَهْرَيْنِ
وَاَكِيدُ	وَيْلَكُمْ	يُرِيدُ	زَيْتُهَا
سَأُصْلِيهِ	عَيْنَيْنِ	نَزِيدَكُمْ	قَوْسَيْنِ

8.3: Long Vowels - Ḥurūf al-Madd | Wāw Madd

Wāw Madd	The Letter	Wāw Madd	The Letter	Wāw Madd	The Letter	Wāw Madd	The Letter
ثُوْ	ثُ	تُوْ	تُ	بُوْ	بُ	اُوْ	ءُ
دُوْ	دُ	خُوْ	خُ	حُوْ	حُ	جُوْ	جُ
سُوْ	سُ	زُوْ	زُ	رُوْ	رُ	ذُوْ	ذُ
طُوْ	طُ	ضُوْ	ضُ	صُوْ	صُ	شُوْ	شُ
فُوْ	فُ	غُوْ	غُ	عُوْ	عُ	ظُوْ	ظُ
مُوْ	مُ	لُوْ	لُ	كُوْ	كُ	قُوْ	قُ
يُوْ	ىُٔ	وُوْ	وُ	هُوْ	هُ	نُوْ	نُ

- Continue to practice these examples with the same breakdown method. Any letters joined with the sukūn must be spelt & read together. For example:

$$"اُوْحِيَ" : اُوْ - حِ - اُوْحِ - يَ = اُوْحِيَ$$

You **must** note down any rules before attempting each and every example.

Annotation: underline every instance of wāw Ḥarf Madd (as shown below)

Example in the end	Example in the middle	Example in the beginning	The Madd Letter
فَاقْرَءُوا	يَئُودُ	اُوحِيَ	اُو
وَيَلْعَبُوا	يَحْسَبُونَ	بُورِكَ	بُو
وَيُؤْتُوا	وَيَأْتُوكُم	تُوعَدُونَ	تُو
لَبِثُوا	تُبْعَثُونَ	- - -	ثُو
وَيَرْجُو	يَخْرُجُونَ	- - -	جُو
فَتَحُوا	نَصِحُونَ	حُوَّتَهُمَا	حُو
- - -	نَخُوضُ	- - -	خُو
لِيَشْهَدُوا	تَفْقِدُونَ	دُونِهٖ	دُو
وَيَحْفَظُوا	يُوعَظُونَ	- - -	ظُو
تَدْعُوا	اَفَتَطْمَعُونَ	عُوقِبَ	عُو

Example in the end	Example in the middle	Example in the beginning	The Madd Letter
لِتَبْلُغُوا	وَيَبْغُوْنَ	ـــ ـــ ـــ	غُوْ
وَاَوْفُوْا	وَيَحْلِفُوْنَ	وَفُوْمِهَا	فُوْ
لِيَذُوْقُوا	يَعْقُوْبَ	قُوْلُوْا	قُوْ
اَشْكُوْا	يُؤْفَكُوْنَ	كُوْنِي	كُوْ
قَالُوْا	جُلُوْدِ	لُوْطُ	لُوْ
تَعَلَمُوْا	ثَمُوْدَ	مُوْسٰى	مُوْ
كَانُوْا	تُحْصِنُوْنَ	نُوْرُ	نُوْ
كَرِهُوْا	يَعْمَهُوْنَ	هُوْدُ	هُوْ
تَلَوْا	دَاوُدُ	وُرِيَ	وُوْ
ـــ ـــ ـــ	بُيُوْتِ	يُوْسُفَ	يُوْ

8.3.a: Wāw Madd & Wāw Sākinah

Wāw Madd	Wāw Sākinah	Wāw Madd	Wāw Sākinah
ثَمُودَ	بِصَوْتِكَ	يَمْشُوْنَ	اَوْجَفْتُمْ
تُحْصِنُوْنَ	يَرْضَوْنَهُ	يَخْرُصُوْنَ	فَاٰبَوْا
يَعْمَهُوْنَ	يُعْطَوْا	لِيُرْضُوْكُمْ	تَعْثَوْا
بُيُوْتِ	لَبِغَوْا	يُعْطُوْا	حَوْلَ
حَافِظُوْنَ	قَوْسَيْنِ	وَيَدْعُوْنَنَا	سَعَوْا
خَاسِرُوْنَ	لَوْلَا	وَيَبْغُوْنُ	فَنَادَوْا
فُوْمِهَا	نَوْمَكُمْ	وَيَحْلِفُوْنَ	اٰذَوْا
قُرُوْنُ	يَنْهَوْنَ	يَعْقُوْبَ	رَوْحِ
يُخَادِعُوْنَ	اٰوَوْا	لِيَكُوْنَ	زَوْجَانِ
مُسْلِمُوْنَ	يَوْمَ	جُلُوْدِ	سَوْفَ

9: Double Vowels | Tanwīn

1. Fathatayn اً   2. Kasratayn ٍ   3. Ḍammatayn ٌ

Tanwīn only appears at the end of certain types of words.

It is recited with a نْ sound.

Ḍammatayn	Kasratayn	Fathatayn	Ḍammatayn	Kasratayn	Fathatayn
بٌ	بٍ	بًا	ءٌ	ءٍ	ءًا
ةٌ	ةٍ	ةً	تٌ	تٍ	تًا
جٌ	جٍ	جًا	ثٌ	ثٍ	ثًا
خٌ	خٍ	خًا	حٌ	حٍ	حًا
ذٌ	ذٍ	ذًا	دٌ	دٍ	دًا
زٌ	زٍ	زًا	رٌ	رٍ	رًا
شٌ	شٍ	شًا	سٌ	سٍ	سًا

- Please note: The Fathatayn always comes with an alif (except with a ة & sometimes ء).
For now, this alif will be a silent bystander.

Ḍammatayn	Kasratayn	Fatḥatayn	Ḍammatayn	Kasratayn	Fatḥatayn
ضٌ	ضٍ	ضًا	صٌ	صٍ	صًا
ظٌ	ظٍ	ظًا	طٌ	طٍ	طًا
غٌ	غٍ	غًا	عٌ	عٍ	عًا
قٌ	قٍ	قًا	فٌ	فٍ	فًا
لٌ	لٍ	لًا	كٌ	كٍ	كًا
نٌ	نٍ	نًا	مٌ	مٍ	مًا
ئٌ	ئٍ	يًا	ةٌ	ةٍ	هًا

- Continue to practice the word examples with the same breakdown method. Any letters joined with the sukūn must be spelt & read together. For example:

$$ \text{اِنْشَاءَ} = \text{ءَ} - \text{اِنْشَا} - \text{شَا} - \text{اِنْ} : "اِنْشَاءَ" $$

You **must** note down any rules before attempting each and every example.

Words with Tanwīn

Ḍammatayn	Kasratayn	Fatḥatayn	The Letter
شَيْءٌ	بِنَبَإٍ	جُزْءًا - اِنْشَاءَ	ء
خُشُبٌ	لَهَبٍ	عَجَبًا	ب
أُخْتٌ	مُحْصَنَاتٍ	وَنَبَاتًا	ت
مُؤْصَدَةٌ	هُمَزَةٍ	بَعُوضَةً	ة
وَحَرْثٌ	حَدِيثٍ	اِنَاثًا	ث
مَوْجٌ	اَمْشَاجٍ	اَفْوَاجًا	ج
نُوحٌ	لَوْحٍ	صِلْحًا	ح
بَرْزَخٌ	بِأَخٍ	شَيْخًا	خ
جُدَدٌ	حَاسِدٍ	اَحَدًا	د
ءَاخِذٌ	يَوْمَئِذٍ	لِوَاذًا	ذ

Ḍammatayn	Kasratayn	Fatḥatayn	The Letter
بَصِيرٌ	وَتَشَاوُرٍ	يُسْرًا	ر
عَزِيزٌ	رِجْزٍ	خُبْزًا	ز
بَأْسٌ	كَأْسٍ	نَفْسًا	س
عَرْشٌ	قُرَيْشٍ	وَرِيشًا	ش
مَرْصُوصٌ	وَنَقْصٍ	قَصَصًا	ص
بَيْضٌ	أَرْضٍ	مَفْرُوضًا	ض
مُحِيطٌ	صِرَاطٍ	نَشْطًا	ط
غِلَاظٌ	مَحْفُوظٍ	اَيْقَاظًا	ظ
سَمِيعٌ	جُوعٍ	زَرْعًا	ع
زَيْغٌ	بَاغٍ	بَلْغًا	غ

Ḍammatayn	Kasratayn	Fatḥatayn	The Letter
مَعْرُوفٌ	خَوْفٍ	صُحُفًا	ف
وَاسْتَبْرَقٌ	غَاسِقٍ	طِبَاقًا	ق
مُبْرَكٌ	فَلَكٍ	دَرَكًا	ك
حَبْلٌ	ضَلَلٍ	لَيْلًا	ل
رَحِيمٌ	تَقْوِيمٍ	قَوْمًا	م
مُبِينٌ	عَدْنٍ	مِسْكِينًا	ن
وُجُوهٌ	اِلهِ	مُشْتَبِهًا	ه
لَغْوٌ	ـــ	رَهْوًا	و
خِزْيٌ	ـــ	بَغْيًا	ي

" بَغْيًا " : بَغْ – يًا = بَغْيًا

10: Shaddah

The Arabic letters with Shaddah ّ

A letter with a shaddah is read with **extra strength**,
by being joined onto the letter before it that has a ḥarakah (vowel).
Stress and hold onto the shaddah letter,
and then pronounce the ḥarakah that comes with the letter.

Shaddah with Ḍammah	Shaddah with Kasra	Shaddah with Fathah	Shaddah with Ḍammah	Shaddah with Kasra	Shaddah with Fathah
تَتُّ	تَتِّ	تَتَّ	تَبُّ	تَبِّ	تَبَّ
تَجُّ	تَجِّ	تَجَّ	تَثُّ	تَثِّ	تَثَّ
تَخُّ	تَخِّ	تَخَّ	تَحُّ	تَحِّ	تَحَّ
تَذُّ	تَذِّ	تَذَّ	تَدُّ	تَدِّ	تَدَّ
تَزُّ	تَزِّ	تَزَّ	تَرُّ	تَرِّ	تَرَّ
تَشُّ	تَشِّ	تَشَّ	تَسُّ	تَسِّ	تَسَّ
تَضُّ	تَضِّ	تَضَّ	تَصُّ	تَصِّ	تَصَّ

Heavy/Light & Light/Heavy Combinations

When a Light Letter joins onto a Heavy Letter, or vice versa,
be mindful not to transfer the quality of one letter onto the other.

Shaddah with Ḍammah	Shaddah with Kasra	Shaddah with Fatḥah	Shaddah with Ḍammah	Shaddah with Kasra	Shaddah with Fatḥah
تَظُّ	تَظِّ	تَظَّ	تَطُّ	تَطِّ	تَطَّ
تَعُّ	تَعِّ	تَعَّ	تَعُّ	تَعِّ	تَعَّ
تَقُّ	تَقِّ	تَقَّ	تَفُّ	تَفِّ	تَفَّ
تَلُّ	تَلِّ	تَلَّ	تَكُّ	تَكِّ	تَكَّ
تَنُّ	تَنِّ	تَنَّ*	تَمُّ	تَمِّ	تَمَّ*
تَوُّ	تَوِّ	تَوَّ	تَهُّ	تَهِّ	تَهَّ
تَيُّ	تَيِّ	تَيَّ			

Ghunnah – Deep Nasal Sound

When a ن or م has a shaddah, you **must always** recite them with a

ghunnah (deep nasal sound) – elongated humming.

- Annotate the ghunnah's with a wavy scribble, as shown, to visually remind
you to make the vibration sound from the nose. [See 10.3 – Pg. 60]

Words with Shaddah

$$"تُبَّعٍ" : تُبْ - عِ = تُبَّعٍ$$

Shaddah with Ḍammah	Shaddah with Kasra	Shaddah with Fatḥah	The Letter
رَبُّكَ	لِحُبِّ	تُبَّعٍ	ب
عَنِتُّم	يُقَتِّلُونَ	يَتَّبِعُ	ت
يَبُثُّ	بَثِّي	فَتَمَثَّلَ	ث
حُجَّ	سُجِّرَت	حُجَّتُهُم	ج
———	وَلِيُمَحِّصَ	شُحَّ	ح
———	يُؤَخِّرَ	سَخَّرَهَا	خ
سَنَشُدُّ	تُحَدِّثُ	تَبَدَّلَ	د
وَتَلَذُّ	يُكَذِّبُونَ	كَذَّبَ	ذ

$$"يُكَذِّبُونَ" : يُ - كَذِّ - يُكَذِّ - بُو - يُكَذِّبُو - نَ = يُكَذِّبُونَ$$

Shaddah with Ḍammah	Shaddah with Kasra	Shaddah with Fatḥah	The Letter
وَالرُّهْبَانِ	بِالْبِرِّ	حَرَّمَ	ر
وَاَعَزُّ	مُزِّقْتُمْ	وَالزَّرْعَ	ز
يَمَسُّهُمْ	فَسَنُيَسِّرُهُ	تَيَسَّرَ	س
وَاَهُشُّ	وَبَشِّرِ	خُشَّعًا	ش
يَقُصُّ	وَحُصِّلَ	فَصَّلْنَا	ص
يَحُضُّ	وَنُفَضِّلُ	وَالْفِضَّةِ	ض
تَخُطُّ	عُطِّلَتْ	تَطَّلِعُ	ط
كَا الظُّلَلِ	يُعَظِّمْ	اِلَّا الظَّنَّ	ظ
يَدُعُّ	تُصَعِّرْ	وَنَعَّمَهُ	ع

$$"تُصَعِّرْ" : تُ - صَعِّرْ = تُصَعِّرْ$$

"خَفَّتْ" : خَفَّتْ

Shaddah with Ḍammah	Shaddah with Kasra	Shaddah with Fatḥah	The Letter
مِنَ التَّعَفُّفِ	يُخَفِّفَ	خَفَّتْ	ف
وَيُحِقُّ	أُقِّتَتْ	وَحُقَّتْ	ق
فَكُّ	فَذَكِّرْ	وَتَوَكَّلْ	ك
تَحِلُّ	فَصِّلْ	فَتَوَلَّ	ل
فَأُمُّ	حُمِّلُوا	ثُمَّ	م
يَظُنُّ	تُفَنِّدُونِ	لَتَرَوُنَّ	ن
يُوَجِّهْهُ	وَيُطَهِّرَكُمْ	وَطَهَّرَكَ	ه
تَخَوُّفٍ	مُسَوِّمِينَ	سَوَّلَتْ	و
يَاَيُّهَا	كَصِّيِّبٍ	تَبَيَّنَ	ي

"لَتَرَوُنَّ" : لَ – تَ – لَتَ – رَ – لَتَرَ – وُنَّ = لَتَرَوُنَّ

10.1: Shaddah with Tanwīn

Shaddah with Ḍammatayn	Shaddah with Kasratayn	Shaddah with Fatḥatayn	The Letter
وَرَبُّ	رَبٍّ	حُبًّا	ب
– – –	فَجٍّ	رَجًّا	ج
وَصَدُّ	مَرَدٍّ	مَدًّا	د
مُسْتَقِرُّ	مُسْتَمِرٍّ	مُصْفَرًّا	ر
– – –	حَظٍّ	حَظًّا	ظ
– – –	أُفٍّ	صَفًّا	ف
حَقُّ	رَقٍّ	شَقًّا	ق
شَكُّ	شَكٍّ	دَكًّا	ك
كُلُّ	وَلِكُلٍّ	اِلَّا	ل

"وَلِكُلٍّ " : وَ – لِ – وَلِ – كُلٍّ = وَلِكُلٍّ

Shaddah with Ḍammatayn	Shaddah with Kasratayn	Shaddah with Fatḥatayn	The Letter
صُمٌّ	غُمٍّ	صُمًّا	م
مُطْمَئِنٌّ	ـــــــ	مَنًّا	ن
لَعَفُوٌّ	عُتُوٍّ	عَفُوًّا	و
لَقَوِيٌّ	خَفِيٍّ	وَلِيًّا	ي

10.2: Shaddah with Ḥurūf al-Madd (Long Vowels)

Shaddah with Wāw Madd	Shaddah with Yā' Madd	Shaddah with Alif Madd	The Letter
تُحِبُّونَ	رَبِّي	صَبَّارٍ	ب
فَجُّوا	نُنْجِّيكَ	نَجَّنَا	ج
يُرَدُّونَ	يَهِدِّي	تَرَدَّى	د
تُحُسُّونَهُمْ	قِسِّيسِينَ	دَسَّاهَا	س

"تُحُسُّونَهُمْ" : تَ – حُسُّو – تَحُسُّو – نَ – تَحُسُّونَ – هُمْ = تَحُسُّونَهُمْ

"نَضَّاخَتَانِ" : نَضَّا – خَ – نَضَّاخَ – تَا – نَضَّاخَتَا – نِ = نَضَّاخَتَانِ

Shaddah with Wāw Madd	Shaddah with Yā' Madd	Shaddah with Alif Madd	The Letter
يَغُضُّونَ	– – –	نَضَّاخَتَانِ	ض
لَمُوَفُّوهُمْ	يُوَفِّيهِمْ	اَفَّاكٍ	ف
زَقُّومٍ	– – –	فَتَلَقَّى	ق
فَكُّ	وَيُزَكِّيهِمْ	اَلْكُّونَ	ك
وَحُلُّوا	مُحَلِّي	جَلَّهَا	ل
لَيُسَمُّونَ	– – –	سَمَّعُونَ	م
وَظَنُّوا	وَيُمْنِيهِمْ	جَنَّتُ	ن
فَحَيُّوا	حُيِّيتُمْ	اَيَّانَ	ي

"لَيُسَمُّونَ" : لَ – يُ – لَيُ – سَمُّو – لَيُسَمُّو – نَ = لَيُسَمُّونَ

10.3 Words with Ghunnah

You **must** note down any rules before attempting each and every example.

حَمَّالَةَ الْحَطَبِ ۝	كَاَنَّهُمْ	اَسَرَّ النَّبِي
اِنَّا لَمَّا طَغَا	لَنُصَدِّقَنَّ	ثُمَّ لَتُنَبَّؤُنَّ
فَاَمَّا مَنْ اُوتِي	هُنَّ اُمُّ الْكِتَابِ	فَاَمَّا تَثْقَفَنَّهُمْ
اِنَّا كُنَّا مَعَكُمْ	اِنَّ الظَّنَّ	فَلَمَّا سَمِعَتْ

وَاَيَّدْنَاهُ   فَلَنُوَلِّيَنَّكَ   قَدَّمَتْ   يَتَكَلَّمُوْنَ   وَغَسَّاقًا

اُمِّيُّوْنَ   يَدَّعُوْنَ   تَلَظَّى   يَقُصُّوْنَ   وَهُزِّي   يَظُنُّوْنَ

يَشَّقَّقُ   ثَجَّاجًا   فَسَوَّاهُنَّ   وَحُقَّتْ   اَهَمَّتْهُمْ

يَكْرَهُهُنَّ   زَقُّوْمٍ   صَبًّا   تُحَمِّلْنَا   عِلِّيُّوْنَ   فَاَتَمَّهُنَّ   فَكَذَّبَ

وَتُوَقِّرُوْهُ   عِلِّيِّيْنَ   اُمِّيُّوْنَ   عُطِّلَتْ   سُيِّرَتْ   لَتَرْكَبُنَّ

11.1: Letter ل in the name of Allāh rule

1. If you see a Faṭḥah or a Ḍammah before the word الله,

the letter ل in the name of الله will be pronounced Heavy.

يَجْعَلُ اللهُ	هُوَ اللهُ	رَسُوْلُ اللّٰهِ
وَاعْبُدُوا اللهَ	سُبْحَانَ اللهِ	وَعَلَى اللهِ

"رَسُوْلُ اللّٰهِ" : رَ – سُوْ – رَسُوْ – لُ اللّٰ – رَسُوْلُ اللّٰ – ﻪِ = رَسُوْلُ اللهِ

2. If you see a kasrah before the word الله,

the letter ل in the name of الله will be pronounced Lightly.

يُهِنِ اللهُ	فِيْ سَبِيْلِ اللهِ	بِاِذْنِ اللهِ
قُلِ اللّٰهُمَّ	بِاٰيَاتِ اللهِ	اِنَّا لِلّٰهِ

- Recall the letter ر rule which is similar in terms of the ḥarakah before the letter determining the heaviness & lightness.

11.2: Ta'awwudh and Tasmiyah

اَعُوْذُ بِاللهِ مِنَ الشَّيْطٰنِ الرَّجِيْمِ

بِسْمِ اللهِ الرَّحْمٰنِ الرَّحِيْمِ

12: Cumulative Review

1. 7 Heavy Letters - O

خ ص ض ط ظ غ ق

How to make a letter heavy - RASF
a. **R**aise the back end of the tongue
b. **A**pply pressure on the makhraj
c. **S**low release of the sound
d. **F**ull Mouth – A build-up of air inside the mouth.

(قِ غِ خِ – Reduces in heaviness)

2. Letter ر Rule

رَ / رُ = Heavy - O

رِ = Light

(If رْ, look at the ḥarakah before it)

3. The ل in the word الله

Fatḥah/Ḍammah before the word الله = Heavy - O

Kasrah before the word الله = Light

4. Throat Letters

خ غ ح ع ء

5. Qalqalah – Bouncing Sound - Q

قُ طُ بُ جُ دُ

*Remember to keep the bounce Heavy for the Heavy Letters (قُ طُ)

6. Hams – Sharp Breathing Sound - H

كُ تُ

*There are also other *Hams* letters.

7. Ḥurūf al-Madd – Stretched Letters - __

a. Fatḥah before Alif — ◌َ / اَ

b. Kasrah before Yā' Sākin — ◌ِ / يِ

c. Ḍammah before Wāw Sākin — ◌ُ / وُ

8. Ghunnah – Deep Nasal Sound - ّ

نّ مّ

13: Nūn Sākin/Tanwīn Rules (4)

- Whenever you see a نْ or a tanwīn (ٌ ٍ ً),

you will have 1 of 4 rules.

- The letter that appears <u>immediately after</u> the

نْ or a tanwīn (ٌ ٍ ً) will determine which one of the 4 rules apply.

1. Iqlāb – "Change" - ب

"If after نْ/tanwīn you see a ب, **CHANGE** the *nūn sound*

into a م with **ghunnah**"

فَاَنْۢبَتْنَا	كَثِيرَةٍ ۢ بِاِذْنِ	مِنْۢ بَعْدِ
ذَنْۢبٍ	لَنَسْفَعًا ۢ بِالنَّاصِيَةِ	
قَوْمًا ۢ بِجَهَالَةٍ	يَنْۢبَغِي	اَنْۢبَتَكُمْ
مِنْۢ بَقْلِهَا	يَوْمَئِذٍ ۢ بِجَهَنَّمَ	
سَمِيعٌ ۢ بَصِيرٌ	مُطْمَئِنٌّ ۢ بِالْاِيمَانِ	

"مِنْۢ بَعْدِ" : مِنْۢ - بَعْ - مِنْۢ بَعْ - دِ = مِنْۢ بَعْدِ

- Annotate the ghunnah with a wavy scribble, as shown, which will visually represent the vibration sound from the nose.

2. Iẓhar – "Clear" – خ غ ح ع ٥ ء

"If after نْ/tanwīn you see any of the THROAT LETTERS,

read the *nūn sound* **CLEARLY**"

عَنْهُمْ	يَوْمَئِذٍ عَلَيْهَا	مِنْ اَهْلِ ^{IZ}
سَلَٰمٌ هِيَ	لِمَنْ خَشِيَ	عَبْدًا اِذَا
اَرْبَعَةٌ حُرُمٌ	كِذْبَةٍ خَاطِئَةٍ	فَسَيُنْغِضُوْنَ
قَوْمٍ هَادٍ	مِنْ عِبَادِنَا	يَوْمَئِذٍ خُشَّعَةٌ

"مِنْ اَهْلِ": مِنْ – اَهْ – مِنْ اَهْ – لِ = مِنْ اَهْلِ

Iqlāb & Iẓhār examples:

كِرَامٍ بَرَرَةٍ	نَارٌ حَامِيَةٌ	يُؤْمِنْ بِرَبِّهِ ^{IQ}
مِنْ بَنِي	اَنْعَمْتَ	غَفُوْرٌ حَلِيْمٌ
يَنْعِقُ	صُمٌّ بُكْمٌ	اَنْ اَعْبُدَ
طَيْرًا اَبَابِيْلَ	وَانْحَرْ	قَرْيَةٍ بَطِرَتْ

"يُؤْمِنْ بِرَبِّهِ": يُؤْ – مِنْ – يُؤْمِنْ – بِ – يُؤْمِنْ بِرَبّ – بِ – رَبّ – يُؤْمِنْ بِرَبّ – ٥ = يُؤْمِنْ بِرَبِّهِ

3. Idghām – "Join" – ل ر - ن م و ي - Types 2*

i. With Ghunnah ن م و ي

"If after نْ/tanwīn you see any of these letters, **JOIN** the letters on either side and read the idghām letter **with ghunnah**."

(Merge the نْ sound)

مِنْ وَّاقٍ	بَرْدًا وَّلَا	فَمَنْ يَّعْمَلْ
وَوَالِدٍ وَّمَا وَلَدَ	وَلَنْ يَّتَمَنَّوْهُ	لِقَوْمٍ يَّعْقِلُوْنَ
فَلَنْ نَّزِيْدَكُمْ	مِنْ مَّسَدٍ	قُلُوْبٌ يَّوْمَئِذٍ

- Annotate the ghunnah with a wavy scribble, as shown, which will visually represent the vibration sound from the nose.

"فَمَنْ يَّعْمَلْ": فَ - مَنْ يَّعْ - فَمَنْ يَّعْ - مَلْ = فَمَنْ يَّعْمَلْ

ii. Without Ghunnah ل ر

"If after نْ/tanwīn you see any of these letters, **JOIN** the letters on either side and read the idghām letter **without ghunnah**."

(Skip the نْ sound)

لَئِنْ لَّمْ	لَرَءُوْفٌ رَّحِيْمٌ	عَنْ رَّبِّهِمْ
فَاقِعٌ لَّوْنُهَا	مِنْ رَّحْمَةِ	خَيْرًا لَّهُمْ

4. Ikhfā' – "Hide" - *All the remaining letters

(ت ث ج د ذ ز س ش ص ض ط ظ ف ق ك)

"If after نْ/tanwīn you see any of the remaining 15 letters,

[1]**HIDE** the نْ sound with a Light Nasal Sound!"

شِهَابٌ ثَاقِبٌ	اَنْ تَتَّقُوْا	مَنْ^{IK} ذَا الَّذِيْ
فَاِنِ انْتَهَوْا	مِنْكُمْ	ظِلًّا ظَلِيْلًا
مِنْ دُوْنِ	دَكًّا دَكًّا	سِلْسِلَةٍ ذَرْعُهَا

"مَنْ ذَا الَّذِيْ": مَنْ – ذَا الَّ – مَنْ ذَا الَّ – ذِيْ = مَنْ ذَا الَّذِيْ

---

[1] Ikhfā' is pronounced by the tongue touching the top palate <u>very lightly</u>, whilst emphasising the pronunciation of the نْ in the nose.

Idghām (2) & Ikhfā' examples:

مُخْلِصًا لَّهُ الدِّيْنَ	جَنَّةً وَّحَرِيْرًا	مِنْ قَبْلِكَ
وَمَنْ يَّكْفُرْ	اَنْ ظَنَّا	قَالَ نُوْحٌ رَّبِّ
بَلْدَةٌ طَيِّبَةٌ	طَلْعٌ نَّضِيْدٌ	رِجَالٌ صَدَقُوْا
قُرْاَنٌ مَّجِيْدٌ	اُمَمٍ مِّمَّنْ مَّعَكَ	عَدَاوَةٌ كَاَنَّهٗ

"مِنْ قَبْلِكَ": مِنْ – قَبْ – مِنْ قَبْ – لِ – مِنْ قَبْلِ – كَ = مِنْ قَبْلِكَ

14: Quick Review

Nūn Sākin/Tanwīn Examples	The Rules
^{IQ} مِنْ بَيْنِ ^{IQ} كِرَامٍ بَرَرَةٍ	**Iqlāb - ب** - **Change** the nūn sākin *sound* into a م with a ghunnah.
^{IZ} مِنْ اَهْلِ ^{IZ} سَلمٌ هِيَ	**Iẓhar – ء ه ع ح غ خ** - **Clear** nūn sākin *sound*.
^{ID} مِنْ يَّوْمِ ^{ID} بَرْدًا وَّلَا	**Idghām with Ghunnah** ي و م ن - **Join** the letters on either side of the nūn sākin *sound*. *Merge the nūn sākin *sound*.
^{ID} مِنْ لَّدُنْ ^{ID} خَيْرًا لَّهُمْ	**Idghām without Ghunnah** ل ر - **Join** the letters on either side of the nūn sākin *sound*. *Skip over the nūn sākin *sound*.
^{IK} مِنْ شَرِّ ^{IK} سِلْسِلَةٍ ذَرْعُهَا	**Ikhfā'** (All the remaining Letters) - **Hide** the nūn sākin *sound* with a light nasal sound.

15: Mīm Sākin Rules (3)

- Whenever you see a مْ you will have 1 of 3 rules.

- In short, مْ will always be read clearly, unless there is a ب or another م after it.

(in which case the مْ will be read with ghunnah)

1. Ikhfā' Shafawī – ب

"If you see a ب after مْ, read the مْ with a ghunnah"

اَجْرَهُمْ بِاَحْسَنِ	فَبَشِّرْهُمْ بِعَذَابٍ
وَ اَنِ احْكُمْ بَيْنَهُمْ	تَرْمِيهِمْ بِحِجَارَةٍ
فَاَصْبَحْتُمْ بِنِعْمَتِهِ	يُحَاسِبْكُمْ بِهِ اللّٰهُ

2. Idghām Shafawī – م

"If you see another م after مْ, read the مّ with a ghunnah"

اَنَّهُمْ مُّفْرَطُوْنَ	رَبِّهِمْ مُّشْفِقُوْنَ
وَلَهُمْ مَّا يَشْتَهُوْنَ	مِنْكُمْ مَّنْ يُرِيْدُ
فَاِنَّ لَكُمْ مَّا سَاَلْتُمْ	وَعَلَيْكُمْ مَّا حُمِّلْتُمْ

3. Iẓhār Shafawī – *All the remaining letters

"If you see any of the remaining letters after مْ, read the مْ clearly."

اَلَمْ نَشْرَحْ	اَمْ جَنَّةُ الْخُلْدِ
وَقَوْلِهِمْ قُلُوبُنَا	حَيْثُ شِئْتُمْ رَغَدًا

Mīm Sākin examples:

- Practice the ikhfā', idghām, and iẓhār shafawī examples.

يَعْلَمَ بِأَنَّ	هُمْ خَيْرٌ	لَهُمْ مَّاذَا
نُسْقِيكُمْ مِّمَّا	وَءَامَنَهُمْ مِّن	اَلَمْ يَجْعَل
يَعْتَصِمْ بِاللَّهِ	ءَاَنْتُمْ اَشَدُّ	رَبَّهُمْ بِهِمْ
اَنَّهُمْ مَّبْعُوثُونَ	لَكُمْ مِّمَّا	وَلَنَبْلُوَنَّكُمْ بِشَيْءٍ
اَيْدِيهِمْ وَمَا	اِلَيْهِمْ قَوْلًا	اَنْتُمْ مُّغْنُونَ
عَلَيْهِمْ رَبَّهُمْ بِذَنْبِهِمْ		لَهُمْ مَّغْفِرَةٌ
اَصَابَتْهُمْ مُّصِيبَةٌ		فَاِذَا هُمْ بِالسَّاهِرَةِ

16: Methods of stopping at the end of Āyāt

a. Read the last letter with a sukūn

Stopping (How to read it)	Normal (How you'll see it)
قُلْ هُوَ اللّهُ اَحَدْ ۝	قُلْ هُوَ اللّهُ اَحَدٌ ۝
وَيَمْنَعُوْنَ الْمَاعُوْنْ ۝	وَيَمْنَعُوْنَ الْمَاعُوْنَ ۝

(Madd 'āriḍ lil-sukūn – Duration = Up to 5 Alifs | refer to 18, pg. 83)

b. Fathatayn, Remove 1 Fathah

Stopping (How to read it)	Normal (How you'll see it)
اِنَّهُمْ يَكِيْدُوْنَ كَيْدَا ۝	اِنَّهُمْ يَكِيْدُوْنَ كَيْدًا ۝
اِنَّ مَعَ الْعُسْرِ يُسْرَا ۝	اِنَّ مَعَ الْعُسْرِ يُسْرًا ۝

*(This rule is called Madd 'Iwaḍ - Duration = 1 Alif)

c. ة changes into a هْ

Stopping (How to read it)	Normal (How you'll see it)
صُحُفًا مُّطَهَّرَهْ ۝ [1]	صُحُفًا مُّطَهَّرَةً ۝
مَا الْقَارِعَهْ ۝	مَا الْقَارِعَةُ ۝

[1] Although the ة holds a <u>fathatayn</u>, the ة is an exception to the Madd 'Iwaḍ rule above.)

16.1: Madd Līn*

Q. What is Madd Līn?
A. "AW" or "AY" sound

(اَوْ بَوْ تَوْ - اَيْ بَيْ تَيْ) – <u>Normally not elongated</u>

- Madd Līn is recited in a unique way when <u>pausing.</u>

- As well as pausing with a sukūn, you also have to <u>elongate</u> the letter, which is normally not stretched.

Q. When do you elongate the Madd Līn?
A. Only when **ALL 3** conditions mentioned below are met.

1. "AW" or "AY" sound.
2. <u>ONLY</u> 1 letter after it
3. At the end of the āyah[1]

Stopping (How to read it - **elongate**)	Normal (How you'll see it)
قُرَيْـشْ ۝	قُرَيْشٍ ۝
وَالصَّيْفْ ۝	وَالصَّيْفِ ۝
هٰذَا الْبَيْتْ ۝	هٰذَا الْبَيْتِ ۝
مِنْ خَوْفْ ۝	مِنْ خَوْفٍ ۝

[1]The Madd Līn rule will also apply if you make a temporary pause in the middle of an āyah.

17.1 Virtues of reciting & memorising the Qurān

اِقْرَءُوا الْقُرْآنَ فَاِنَّهُ يَأْتِي يَوْمَ الْقِيَامَةِ شَفِيعًا لِأَصْحَابِهِ

1. **"Recite the Qurān, for on the Day of Resurrection it will come as an intercessor for its companion."** – Sahih Muslim

خَيْرُكُمْ مَنْ تَعَلَّمَ الْقُرْآنَ وَعَلَّمَهُ

2. **"The best amongst you are those who learn the Qurān and teach it."** – Sahih al-Bukhari

مَثَلُ الَّذِي يَقْرَأُ الْقُرْآنَ وَهُوَ حَافِظٌ لَهُ مَعَ السَّفَرَةِ الْكِرَامِ الْبَرَرَةِ وَمَثَلُ الَّذِي يَقْرَأُ وَهُوَ يَتَعَاهَدُهُ وَهُوَ عَلَيْهِ شَدِيدٌ فَلَهُ اَجْرَانِ

3. **"The example of those who recites the Qurān and memorise it, is that of one who is with the 'righteous and noble scribes' (80:15); and the example of one who recites the Qurān with great difficulty, is that of one who receives a double reward."** – Sahih al-Bukhari

لَا حَسَدَ اِلَّا عَلَى اثْنَتَيْنِ رَجُلٌ آتَاهُ اللّٰهُ هَذَا الْكِتَابَ فَقَامَ بِهِ آنَاءَ اللَّيْلِ وَآنَاءَ النَّهَارِ وَرَجُلٌ آتَاهُ اللّٰهُ مَالًا فَتَصَدَّقَ بِهِ آنَاءَ اللَّيْلِ وَآنَاءَ النَّهَارِ

4. **"There is no envy except in two cases: a man whom Allāh has given this Book so he stands to recite it during the night and the day, and a man whom Allāh has given wealth and he spends it during the night and day."** - Sahih al-Bukhari

مَنْ قَرَأَ حَرْفًا مِنْ كِتَابِ اللّٰهِ فَلَهُ بِهِ حَسَنَةٌ وَالْحَسَنَةُ بِعَشْرِ اَمْثَالِهَا لَا اَقُولُ الم حَرْفٌ وَلَكِنْ اَلِفٌ حَرْفٌ وَلَامٌ حَرْفٌ وَمِيمٌ حَرْفٌ

5. **"Whoever recites a letter from the Book of Allāh, he will receive one good deed as ten good deeds like it. I do not say that alif-lam-mīm is one letter, but rather alif is a letter, lam is a letter, and mīm is a letter."** – Sunan at-Tirmidhi

يُقَالُ لِصَاحِبِ الْقُرْآنِ: اِقْرَأْ وَارْتَقِ وَرَتِّلْ كَمَا كُنْتَ تُرَتِّلُ فِي الدُّنْيَا فَاِنَّ مَنْزِلَكَ عِنْدَ آخِرِ آيَةٍ تَقْرَؤُهَا

6. **"It will be said to the companion of the Qurān: Recite and ascend as you recited in the world, for your rank is determined by the last verse you recite."** – Sunan at-Tirmidhi

17.2 Etiquettes of Qurānic Reading - [Tilāwah]

Certain etiquettes are preferable, whilst other etiquettes need to be observed by a person who intends to engage in the recitation of the Qurān.

Before commencing recitation, the person should:

- **Perform Wudhu.** It is not permissible to touch the Qurān without wudhu.

- **Use a Miswak** and ensure that the mouth is cleansed of any offensive smell such as garlic.

- **Show the greatest of respect to the Qurān.** The person should not sit positioned higher than the Qurān and should place the Qurān on an elevated place (desk, cushion).

- **Sit facing the Qiblah** and in a dignified manner.

- **Apply fragrance** (ittr).

- **Intend to please only Allāh** ﷻ.

- **Read Salawāt upon our final Prophet** ﷺ.

- **Recite the ta'awwudh and tasmiyah** (refer to pg. 61).

During the recitation, the person should:

- Read the Qurān with undivided attention and as if s/he is in Allāh's ﷻ presence.

- Read in such a manner that s/he is aware that Allāh ﷻ is listening to his/her recital.

- Read the Qurān in a melodious voice as this is encouraged in the ahādith.

- Read the Qurān correctly according to the rules of tajwīd.
  Reading hastily may probably result in incorrect recitation.

- Respond to the subject matter of the Qurān accordingly. When reciting ayāt of mercy and retribution, seek Allāh's mercy and forgiveness respectively.

QURĀN PRACTICE

- To consolidate all that you have learnt, it is **<u>absolutely vital</u>** to continue practicing with the breakdown method.

- Up to this point, we have only been practicing 1, 2, or 3 words at a time.

- As we take a leap into reading directly from the Qurān, it is imperative that we continue practicing in a way that will help with fluency and proficiency.

- The letter-by-letter breakdown method may seem tedious, yet, it is necessary. It is required to reach a high level of reading. This will help instil a thorough understanding of the rules of recitation with confidence.

Therefore:

- Before you attempt any āyah, first you **must** <u>figure out & note down</u> (using a pencil) all of the rules you find.
(The 'key' is on the next two pages)

- Once you have noted all of the rules, you should attempt the āyah with the breakdown method.

- Do not move onto the next āyah until you are reciting the previous āyah confidently and fluently whilst applying all the rules.

- Below is a table of the symbols you will need to annotate to remind you to apply the necessary rules.

Rule	Symbol
Heavy Letter	**O**
Qalqalah	**Q**
Hams	**H**
Ḥurūf al-Madd (Including other stretches)	—
Ghunnah	⸮
Iqlāb	IQ ⸮
Iẓhār	IZ
Idghām with Ghunnah	ID ⸮
Idghām without Ghunnah	ID
Ikhfāʾ	IK ⸮

Ikhfā' Shafawī	IK-S
Idghām Shafawī	ID-S
Iẓhār Shafawī	(Leave Blank)
Madd Muttaṣil (refer to 17.1, Pg. 83)	5 ___
Madd Munfaṣil (refer to 17.2, Pg. 84)	3 ___

First annotate and then attempt this passage from the Qurān - Surah Ma'ārij, as described on page 75.

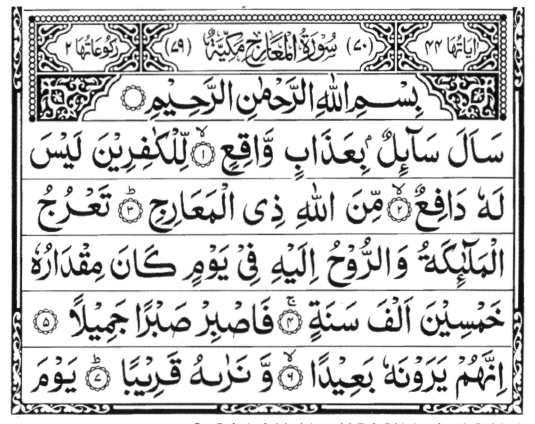

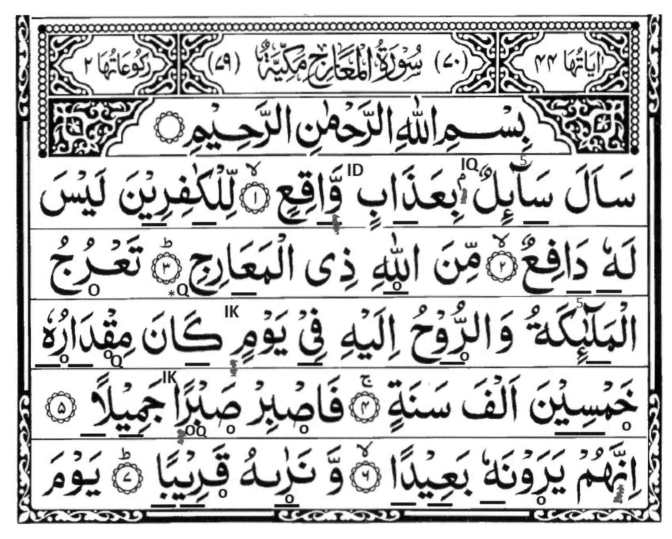

Check your attempt alongside the above.

Did you miss out any rules?

Try a new surah on the next page.

Suratul Fath - The Victory

سُوْرَةُ الْفَتْحِ مَدَنِيَّةٌ (١١١) ﴿٢٨﴾ اٰيَاتُهَا ٢٩ رُكُوْعَاتُهَا ٣

بِسْمِ اللّٰهِ الرَّحْمٰنِ الرَّحِيْمِ ۞

اِنَّا فَتَحْنَا لَكَ فَتْحًا مُّبِيْنًا ۙ ١ لِّيَغْفِرَ لَكَ اللّٰهُ مَا

تَقَدَّمَ مِنْ ذَنْبِكَ وَمَا تَأَخَّرَ وَيُتِمَّ نِعْمَتَهٗ عَلَيْكَ

وَيَهْدِيَكَ صِرَاطًا مُّسْتَقِيْمًا ۙ ٢ وَّيَنْصُرَكَ اللّٰهُ

نَصْرًا عَزِيْزًا ٣ هُوَ الَّذِيْٓ اَنْزَلَ السَّكِيْنَةَ فِيْ

قُلُوْبِ الْمُؤْمِنِيْنَ لِيَزْدَادُوْٓا اِيْمَانًا مَّعَ اِيْمَانِهِمْ ط

وَلِلّٰهِ جُنُوْدُ السَّمٰوٰتِ وَالْاَرْضِ ط وَكَانَ اللّٰهُ عَلِيْمًا

حَكِيْمًا ۙ ٤ لِّيُدْخِلَ الْمُؤْمِنِيْنَ وَالْمُؤْمِنٰتِ جَنّٰتٍ

تَجْرِيْ مِنْ تَحْتِهَا الْاَنْهٰرُ خٰلِدِيْنَ فِيْهَا وَيُكَفِّرَ

عَنْهُمْ سَيِّاٰتِهِمْ ط وَكَانَ ذٰلِكَ عِنْدَ اللّٰهِ فَوْزًا

عَظِيْمًا ۙ ٥

سُوْرَةُ الْفَتْحِ مَدَنِيَّةٌ (٤٨) رُكُوْعَاتُهَا ٤ (١١١) اٰیَاتُهَا ٢٩

بِسْمِ اللّٰهِ الرَّحْمٰنِ الرَّحِيْمِ ۝

اِنَّا فَتَحْنَا لَكَ فَتْحًا مُّبِيْنًا ۝ لِّيَغْفِرَ لَكَ اللّٰهُ مَا

تَقَدَّمَ مِنْ ذَنْۢبِكَ وَمَا تَاَخَّرَ وَيُتِمَّ نِعْمَتَهٗ عَلَيْكَ

وَيَهْدِيَكَ صِرَاطًا مُّسْتَقِيْمًا ۝ وَّيَنْصُرَكَ اللّٰهُ

نَصْرًا عَزِيْزًا ۝ هُوَ الَّذِيْٓ اَنْزَلَ السَّكِيْنَةَ فِيْ

قُلُوْبِ الْمُؤْمِنِيْنَ لِيَزْدَادُوْٓا اِيْمَانًا مَّعَ اِيْمَانِهِمْ ۗ

وَلِلّٰهِ جُنُوْدُ السَّمٰوٰتِ وَالْاَرْضِ ۗ وَكَانَ اللّٰهُ عَلِيْمًا

حَكِيْمًا ۝ لِّيُدْخِلَ الْمُؤْمِنِيْنَ وَالْمُؤْمِنٰتِ جَنّٰتٍ

تَجْرِيْ مِنْ تَحْتِهَا الْاَنْهٰرُ خٰلِدِيْنَ فِيْهَا وَيُكَفِّرَ

عَنْهُمْ سَيِّاٰتِهِمْ ۗ وَكَانَ ذٰلِكَ عِنْدَ اللّٰهِ فَوْزًا

عَظِيْمًا ۝

<u>Suratul Fātiḥah – The Opening</u>

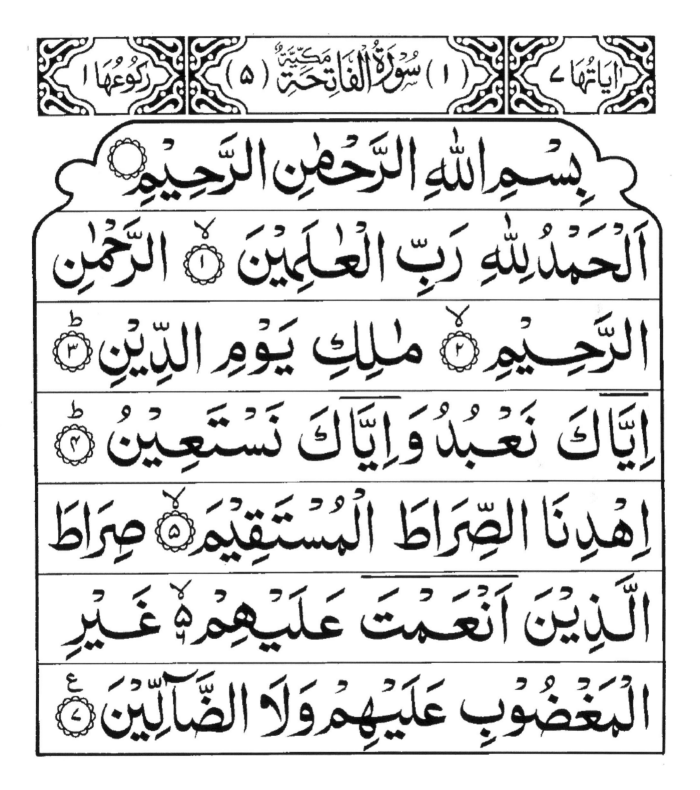

Āyatul Kursī – The Throne

اَللّٰهُ لَآ اِلٰهَ اِلَّا هُوَ اَلْحَیُّ الْقَیُّوْمُ ۚ لَا تَاْخُذُهٗ

سِنَةٌ وَّلَا نَوْمٌ ؕ لَهٗ مَا فِی السَّمٰوٰتِ وَمَا فِی الْاَرْضِ ؕ

مَنْ ذَا الَّذِیْ یَشْفَعُ عِنْدَهٗۤ اِلَّا بِاِذْنِهٖ ؕ یَعْلَمُ

مَا بَیْنَ اَیْدِیْهِمْ وَمَا خَلْفَهُمْ ۚ وَلَا یُحِیْطُوْنَ

بِشَیْءٍ مِّنْ عِلْمِهٖۤ اِلَّا بِمَا شَآءَ ۚ وَسِعَ كُرْسِیُّهُ

السَّمٰوٰتِ وَالْاَرْضَ ۚ وَلَا یَـُٔوْدُهٗ حِفْظُهُمَا ۚ

وَهُوَ الْعَلِیُّ الْعَظِیْمُ ۝٢٥٥

18: Madd Far'ī

- Madd Far'ī is when there is a **hamzah, sukūn** or **shaddah** <u>after</u> the Ḥurūf al-Madd.

- Madd Far'ī is split into four categories:

1	**Madd Muttaṣil**
2	**Madd Munfaṣil**
3	**Madd Lāzim**
4	**Madd 'āriḍ lil-sukūn*** *(refer to 16a, pg. 71)*

18.1: Madd (Wājib) Muttaṣil

- When a ء appears after a Ḥarf Madd in the **same word**

- The duration of Madd Muttaṣil is elongated up to **5 times longer** than a regular Ḥarf Madd.

Madd Muttaṣil with Wāw Madd	Madd Muttaṣil with Yā' Madd	Madd Muttaṣil with Alif Madd
بِالسَّوٓءِ	خَطِيٓئَتُهُ	جَآءَ

(Madd Muttaṣil – Duration = 5 Alifs)

18.2: Madd Munfaṣil

- When a ء appears after a Ḥarf Madd in the **following word**

- The duration of Madd Munfaṣil can be elongated up to **3 times longer** than a regular Ḥarf Madd.

Madd Munfaṣil with Wāw Madd	Madd Munfaṣil with Yā' Madd	Madd Munfaṣil with Alif Madd
قَالُوٓا اَنُؤۡمِنُ	فِىٓ اَنۡفُسِكُمۡ	مَآ اَنۡزَلۡنَا

(Madd Munfaṣil – Duration = Up to 3 Alifs)

18.3: Madd Lāzim

- When a Ḥarf Madd is **followed by** a ْ or a ّ in the **same word**.

- The duration of Madd Lāzim is elongated **5 times longer** than a regular Ḥarf Madd.

Madd Lāzim with Sukūn	Madd Lāzim with Shaddah	Madd Lāzim with Shaddah
آلۡـَٔنَ [1]	اَلۡحَآقَّةُ	وَ لَا الضَّآلِّينَ

(Madd Lāzim – Duration = 5 Alifs)

[1]Madd Lāzim with a sukūn appears only twice in the Qurān – Only with this word.

19: Ḥurūf Muqaṭṭaʿah

- Certain Surahs in the Qurān begin with letters which are collectively known as Ḥurūf Muqaṭṭaʿah.

- The Ḥurūf Muqaṭṭaʿah are to be recited as they are written.*

- The length of the madd (stretch) is determined by how they are spelt out – See examples below

Pronounced as	Example
اَلِف لَآمُ مِّيمْ	الٓمَّ
حَا مِّيمْ	حٰمٓ
طَا سِيْن مِّيمْ	طٰسٓمَّ
طَا هَا	طٰهٰ
يَا سِيْن	يٰسٓ

20: Tajwīd Quiz!

1. What does the word Tajwīd mean?

………………………………………………………………………..(1 Point)

2. What does Laḥn Jalī mean?

…………………………………………………………………….(1 Point)

3. What does Laḥn Khafī mean?

…………………………………………………………………..(1 Point)

4. Explain what would be regarded as Laḥn Jalī in recitation.

……………………………………………………………………..

………………………………………………………………(3 Points)

5. Explain what would be regarded as Laḥn Khafī in recitation.

……………………………………………………………………..

………………………………………………………………(3 Points)

6. What does the word Makhraj mean?

……………………………………………………………..(1 Point)

7. List the 7 Heavy Letters.

………   ………   ………   ………   ………   ………   ……… (2 Points)

8. How do we pronounce the Heavy Letters?

a. ………………………………………………………………………………………………

b. ………………………………………………………………………………………………

c. ………………………………………………………………………………………………

d. ……………………………………………………………………………………...(4 Points)

9. Write down the 6 letters of the throat.

…………..   ………….. - Top of the throat

…………..   ………….. - Middle of the throat

…………..   ………….. - Bottom of the throat   (6 Points)

10. What are the names of the 3 Ḥarakāt (short vowels) in Arabic?

…………………….   ……………………….   …………………….. (1 Point)

11. What will the ا (Alif) be considered as when it holds any of the Ḥarakāt?

…………………………………………………………………..…(1 Point)

12. What is the meaning of the word Qalqalah?

…………………………………………………………………..…(1 Point)

13. On which letters does the Qalqalah rule apply?

…………   …………   …………   …………   ………… (5 Points)

14. Explain how you can determine the heaviness or the lightness of the letter ر when it is holding a Sukūn.

………………………………………………………………………

……………………………………………………………….(2 Points)

15. Explain how the letters of hams are pronounced.

………………………………………………………………………

……………………………………………………………….(2 Points)

16. What are the Ḥurūf al-Madd?

a. ....

b. ....

c. ....(3 Points)

17. What does the word Ghunnah mean?

....(1 Point)

18. When holding a shaddah, on which 2 letters does the Ghunnah rule always apply?

....   (1 Point)

19. When should you pronounce the word الله lightly?

....(1 Point)

20. When the letter خ follows a نْ, which tajwīd rule must be exercised?

....(1 Point)

21. When would the Ghunnah apply on the letter ي or the letter و?

....(2 Points)

22. What are the letters of Idghām with Ghunnah?

....   (2 Points)

23. Explain the Ikhfā' Shafawī rule.

....

....(2 Points)

24. Explain the process that occurs when applying the Iqlāb rule.

....

....(2 Points)

25. Why does the نْ and Tanwīn have the same rules?

....

....(1 Point)

26. Explain what you must do when you end an āyah on a word that has a Fatḥatayn.

....

....(2 Points)

27. How would you stop at an āyah that ends with a ﺓ?

....(2 Points)

28. How would you stop at an āyah that ends with a Ḥarf Madd?

....(1 Point)

29. What are the 3 conditions for the Madd Līn to apply?

a. ....

b. ....

c. ....(3 Points)

30. After the Ḥarf Madd,

a. Madd Muttaṣil is when the ء appears in the .... word

b. Madd Munfaṣil is when the ء appears in the .... word
(2 Points)

Suratul Kahf

بِسْمِ اللهِ الرَّحْمٰنِ الرَّحِيْمِ ۝

اَلْحَمْدُ لِلّٰهِ الَّذِيْٓ اَنْزَلَ عَلٰى عَبْدِهِ الْكِتٰبَ وَلَمْ يَجْعَلْ لَّهٗ عِوَجًا ۝ قَيِّمًا لِّيُنْذِرَ بَأْسًا شَدِيْدًا مِّنْ لَّدُنْهُ وَيُبَشِّرَ الْمُؤْمِنِيْنَ الَّذِيْنَ يَعْمَلُوْنَ الصّٰلِحٰتِ اَنَّ لَهُمْ اَجْرًا حَسَنًا ۝ مَّاكِثِيْنَ فِيْهِ اَبَدًا ۝ وَّيُنْذِرَ الَّذِيْنَ قَالُوا اتَّخَذَ اللهُ وَلَدًا ۝ مَا لَهُمْ بِهٖ مِنْ عِلْمٍ وَّلَا لِاٰبَآئِهِمْ ۚ كَبُرَتْ كَلِمَةً تَخْرُجُ مِنْ اَفْوَاهِهِمْ ؕ اِنْ يَّقُوْلُوْنَ اِلَّا كَذِبًا ۝ فَلَعَلَّكَ بَاخِعٌ

نَّفْسَكَ عَلَىٰٓ اٰثَارِهِمْ اِنْ لَّمْ يُؤْمِنُوْا بِهٰذَا الْحَدِيْثِ

اَسَفًا ۞ اِنَّا جَعَلْنَا مَا عَلَى الْاَرْضِ زِيْنَةً لَّهَا

لِنَبْلُوَهُمْ اَيُّهُمْ اَحْسَنُ عَمَلًا ۞ وَاِنَّا لَجٰعِلُوْنَ مَا

عَلَيْهَا صَعِيْدًا جُرُزًا ۞ اَمْ حَسِبْتَ اَنَّ اَصْحٰبَ الْكَهْفِ

وَالرَّقِيْمِ كَانُوْا مِنْ اٰيٰتِنَا عَجَبًا ۞ اِذْ اَوَى الْفِتْيَةُ

اِلَى الْكَهْفِ فَقَالُوْا رَبَّنَآ اٰتِنَا مِنْ لَّدُنْكَ

رَحْمَةً وَّهَيِّئْ لَنَا مِنْ اَمْرِنَا رَشَدًا ۞

Suratul Mulk

بِسْمِ اللّٰهِ الرَّحْمٰنِ الرَّحِيْمِ ۝

تَبٰرَكَ الَّذِىْ بِيَدِهِ الْمُلْكُ ۖ وَهُوَ عَلٰى كُلِّ شَىْءٍ قَدِيْرٌ ۝ الَّذِىْ خَلَقَ الْمَوْتَ وَالْحَيٰوةَ لِيَبْلُوَكُمْ اَيُّكُمْ اَحْسَنُ عَمَلًا ۗ وَهُوَ الْعَزِيْزُ الْغَفُوْرُ ۝ الَّذِىْ خَلَقَ سَبْعَ سَمٰوٰتٍ طِبَاقًا ۗ مَا تَرٰى فِىْ خَلْقِ الرَّحْمٰنِ مِنْ تَفٰوُتٍ ۖ فَارْجِعِ الْبَصَرَ ۙ هَلْ تَرٰى مِنْ فُطُوْرٍ ۝ ثُمَّ ارْجِعِ الْبَصَرَ كَرَّتَيْنِ يَنْقَلِبْ اِلَيْكَ الْبَصَرُ خَاسِئًا وَّهُوَ حَسِيْرٌ ۝ وَلَقَدْ زَيَّنَّا السَّمَآءَ الدُّنْيَا بِمَصَابِيْحَ وَجَعَلْنٰهَا رُجُوْمًا لِّلشَّيٰطِيْنِ وَاَعْتَدْنَا لَهُمْ عَذَابَ السَّعِيْرِ ۝ وَلِلَّذِيْنَ كَفَرُوْا بِرَبِّهِمْ عَذَابُ جَهَنَّمَ ۗ وَبِئْسَ الْمَصِيْرُ ۝ اِذَآ اُلْقُوْا فِيْهَا سَمِعُوْا لَهَا شَهِيْقًا وَّهِىَ تَفُوْرُ ۝ تَكَادُ تَمَيَّزُ مِنَ الْغَيْظِ ۗ

كُلَّمَآ أُلْقِىَ فِيهَا فَوْجٌ سَأَلَهُمْ خَزَنَتُهَآ أَلَمْ يَأْتِكُمْ

نَذِيرٌ ۝ قَالُوا بَلَىٰ قَدْ جَآءَنَا نَذِيرٌ فَكَذَّبْنَا

وَقُلْنَا مَا نَزَّلَ اللَّهُ مِن شَىْءٍ إِنْ أَنتُمْ إِلَّا فِى

ضَلَٰلٍ كَبِيرٍ ۝ وَقَالُوا لَوْ كُنَّا نَسْمَعُ أَوْ نَعْقِلُ مَا

كُنَّا فِىٓ أَصْحَٰبِ السَّعِيرِ ۝ فَاعْتَرَفُوا بِذَنۢبِهِمْ

فَسُحْقًا لِّأَصْحَٰبِ السَّعِيرِ ۝ إِنَّ الَّذِينَ يَخْشَوْنَ

رَبَّهُم بِالْغَيْبِ لَهُم مَّغْفِرَةٌ وَأَجْرٌ كَبِيرٌ ۝ وَأَسِرُّوا

قَوْلَكُمْ أَوِ اجْهَرُوا بِهِ إِنَّهُ عَلِيمٌ بِذَاتِ الصُّدُورِ ۝

أَلَا يَعْلَمُ مَنْ خَلَقَ وَهُوَ اللَّطِيفُ الْخَبِيرُ ۝ هُوَ

الَّذِى جَعَلَ لَكُمُ الْأَرْضَ ذَلُولًا فَامْشُوا فِى مَنَاكِبِهَا

وَكُلُوا مِن رِّزْقِهِ وَإِلَيْهِ النُّشُورُ ۝ ءَأَمِنتُم مَّن

فِى السَّمَآءِ أَن يَخْسِفَ بِكُمُ الْأَرْضَ فَإِذَا هِىَ تَمُورُ ۝

أَمْ أَمِنتُم مَّن فِى السَّمَآءِ أَن يُرْسِلَ عَلَيْكُمْ

حَاصِبًا ۖ فَسَتَعْلَمُوْنَ كَيْفَ نَذِيْرِ ﴿١٤﴾ وَلَقَدْ كَذَّبَ

الَّذِيْنَ مِنْ قَبْلِهِمْ فَكَيْفَ كَانَ نَكِيْرِ ﴿١٨﴾ اَوَلَمْ يَرَوْا

اِلَى الطَّيْرِ فَوْقَهُمْ صٰٓفّٰتٍ وَّيَقْبِضْنَ ۘ مَا يُمْسِكُهُنَّ

اِلَّا الرَّحْمٰنُ ۚ اِنَّهٗ بِكُلِّ شَىْءٍ ۢ بَصِيْرٌ ﴿١٩﴾ اَمَّنْ هٰذَا

الَّذِيْ هُوَ جُنْدٌ لَّكُمْ يَنْصُرُكُمْ مِّنْ دُوْنِ الرَّحْمٰنِ ۚ

اِنِ الْكٰفِرُوْنَ اِلَّا فِيْ غُرُوْرٍ ﴿٢٠﴾ اَمَّنْ هٰذَا الَّذِيْ

يَرْزُقُكُمْ اِنْ اَمْسَكَ رِزْقَهٗ ۚ بَلْ لَّجُّوْا فِيْ عُتُوٍّ

وَّنُفُوْرٍ ﴿٢١﴾ اَفَمَنْ يَّمْشِيْ مُكِبًّا عَلٰى وَجْهِهٖٓ اَهْدٰىٓ

اَمَّنْ يَّمْشِيْ سَوِيًّا عَلٰى صِرَاطٍ مُّسْتَقِيْمٍ ﴿٢٢﴾ قُلْ

هُوَ الَّذِيْٓ اَنْشَاَكُمْ وَجَعَلَ لَكُمُ السَّمْعَ وَالْاَبْصَارَ

وَالْاَفْئِدَةَ ۖ قَلِيْلًا مَّا تَشْكُرُوْنَ ﴿٢٣﴾ قُلْ هُوَ الَّذِيْ

ذَرَاَكُمْ فِي الْاَرْضِ وَاِلَيْهِ تُحْشَرُوْنَ ﴿٢٤﴾ وَيَقُوْلُوْنَ

مَتٰى هٰذَا الْوَعْدُ اِنْ كُنْتُمْ صٰدِقِيْنَ ﴿٢٥﴾ قُلْ

إِنَّمَا الْعِلْمُ عِنْدَ اللَّهِ وَإِنَّمَا أَنَا نَذِيرٌ مُّبِينٌ ﴿٢٦﴾

فَلَمَّا رَأَوْهُ زُلْفَةً سِيٓئَتْ وُجُوهُ الَّذِينَ كَفَرُوا

وَقِيلَ هَذَا الَّذِي كُنْتُمْ بِهِ تَدَّعُونَ ﴿٢٧﴾ قُلْ

أَرَءَيْتُمْ إِنْ أَهْلَكَنِيَ اللَّهُ وَمَنْ مَّعِيَ أَوْ رَحِمَنَا

فَمَنْ يُجِيرُ الْكَافِرِينَ مِنْ عَذَابٍ أَلِيمٍ ﴿٢٨﴾ قُلْ هُوَ

الرَّحْمَنُ ءَامَنَّا بِهِ وَعَلَيْهِ تَوَكَّلْنَا فَسَتَعْلَمُونَ

مَنْ هُوَ فِي ضَلَالٍ مُّبِينٍ ﴿٢٩﴾ قُلْ أَرَءَيْتُمْ إِنْ أَصْبَحَ

مَاؤُكُمْ غَوْرًا فَمَنْ يَأْتِيكُمْ بِمَآءٍ مَّعِينٍ ﴿٣٠﴾

Suratun Naba'

بِسْمِ اللهِ الرَّحْمٰنِ الرَّحِيْمِ ۝

عَمَّ يَتَسَآءَلُوْنَ ۝١ عَنِ النَّبَاِ الْعَظِيْمِ ۝٢ الَّذِىْ هُمْ فِيْهِ

مُخْتَلِفُوْنَ ۝٣ كَلَّا سَيَعْلَمُوْنَ ۝٤ ثُمَّ كَلَّا سَيَعْلَمُوْنَ ۝٥ اَلَمْ نَجْعَلِ

الْاَرْضَ مِهٰدًا ۝٦ وَّالْجِبَالَ اَوْتَادًا ۝٧ وَّخَلَقْنٰكُمْ اَزْوَاجًا ۝٨

وَّجَعَلْنَا نَوْمَكُمْ سُبَاتًا ۝٩ وَّجَعَلْنَا الَّيْلَ لِبَاسًا ۝١٠ وَّجَعَلْنَا

النَّهَارَ مَعَاشًا ۝١١ وَّبَنَيْنَا فَوْقَكُمْ سَبْعًا شِدَادًا ۝١٢ وَّجَعَلْنَا

سِرَاجًا وَّهَّاجًا ۝١٣ وَّاَنْزَلْنَا مِنَ الْمُعْصِرٰتِ مَآءً ثَجَّاجًا

۝١٤ لِّنُخْرِجَ بِهٖ حَبًّا وَّنَبَاتًا ۝١٥ وَّجَنّٰتٍ اَلْفَافًا ۝١٦ اِنَّ يَوْمَ الْفَصْلِ

كَانَ مِيْقَاتًا ۝١٧ يَّوْمَ يُنْفَخُ فِى الصُّوْرِ فَتَأْتُوْنَ اَفْوَاجًا ۝١٨ وَّ

فُتِحَتِ السَّمَآءُ فَكَانَتْ اَبْوَابًا ۝١٩ وَّسُيِّرَتِ الْجِبَالُ فَكَانَتْ

سَرَابًا ۝٢٠ اِنَّ جَهَنَّمَ كَانَتْ مِرْصَادًا ۝٢١ لِّلطَّاغِيْنَ مَاٰبًا

۝٢٢ لّٰبِثِيْنَ فِيْهَآ اَحْقَابًا ۝٢٣ لَا يَذُوْقُوْنَ فِيْهَا بَرْدًا وَّلَا شَرَابًا ۝٢٤

اِلَّا حَمِيْمًا وَّغَسَّاقًا ۩۲۵ جَزَآءً وِّفَاقًا ۩۲۶ اِنَّهُمْ كَانُوْا لَا يَرْجُوْنَ

حِسَابًا ۩۲۷ وَّكَذَّبُوْا بِاٰيٰتِنَا كِذَّابًا ۩۲۸ وَكُلَّ شَيْءٍ اَحْصَيْنٰهُ

كِتٰبًا ۩۲۹ فَذُوْقُوْا فَلَنْ نَّزِيْدَكُمْ اِلَّا عَذَابًا ۩۳۰ اِنَّ لِلْمُتَّقِيْنَ

مَفَازًا ۩۳۱ حَدَآئِقَ وَاَعْنَابًا ۩۳۲ وَّكَوَاعِبَ اَتْرَابًا ۩۳۳ وَّكَأْسًا

دِهَاقًا ۩۳۴ لَا يَسْمَعُوْنَ فِيْهَا لَغْوًا وَّلَا كِذَّابًا ۩۳۵ جَزَآءً مِّنْ رَّبِّكَ عَطَآءً

حِسَابًا ۩۳۶ رَّبِّ السَّمٰوٰتِ وَالْاَرْضِ وَمَا بَيْنَهُمَا الرَّحْمٰنِ لَا يَمْلِكُوْنَ

مِنْهُ خِطَابًا ۩۳۷ يَوْمَ يَقُوْمُ الرُّوْحُ وَالْمَلٰٓئِكَةُ صَفًّا ۖ لَا يَتَكَلَّمُوْنَ

اِلَّا مَنْ اَذِنَ لَهُ الرَّحْمٰنُ وَقَالَ صَوَابًا ۩۳۸ ذٰلِكَ الْيَوْمُ الْحَقُّ ۚ فَمَنْ

شَآءَ اتَّخَذَ اِلٰى رَبِّهٖ مَاٰبًا ۩۳۹ اِنَّا اَنْذَرْنٰكُمْ عَذَابًا قَرِيْبًا ۖ يَّوْمَ يَنْظُرُ

الْمَرْءُ مَا قَدَّمَتْ يَدٰهُ وَيَقُوْلُ الْكٰفِرُ يٰلَيْتَنِيْ كُنْتُ تُرٰابًا ۩۴۰

Qurānic Insights endeavours to continue providing educational content through our online courses and webinars for <u>FREE</u>.
Utilising this platform, we hope to reach out to the worldwide ummah.

We work towards providing services accessible to all, inspiring obedience to our Creator and following in the footsteps of His final Messenger ﷺ.

Become a Qurānic Insights supporter with your du'ā & participation.
If you would like more information on our projects or to contribute financially towards our growing costs, please get in touch.

<u>Contribute here:</u>
- One-off contribution:
PayPal: www.paypal.com/paypalme/Qurānicinsights

- To set up a <u>monthly contribution</u> as a **ṣadaqah jāriyah**, please contact us via email or phone/WhatsApp.

Website: www.QuranicInsights.com
Email: info@Quranicinsights.com
Contact: +44 7741 478 813
YouTube: Quranic Insights (subscribe)
Facebook: facebook.com/QuranicInsights
Instagram: instagram.com/Quranic_insights

*Check out our YouTube channel for videos demonstrating how to navigate through this book using the unique Qurānic Insights Method.

Printed in Poland
by Amazon Fulfillment
Poland Sp. z o.o., Wrocław

86251580R00058